FIRST AWAKENING:

A Spiritual Memoir

(adapted from *Dialogues With the Lord of Time*)

An Appreciation

by Anne Steinemann, PhD

John Roger Barrie takes us on a transcendent spiritual journey with his brilliant and breathtaking autobiographical memoir. This is the work of a spiritual prodigy and perspicacious mystic, who writes of encountering God as a teenager. His insights and foresights are captivating and compelling. He brings us to the depths of the human soul and to the heights of heaven.

As a lifelong Catholic, John's experiences center on Jesus. While remaining solidly a Christian, he later embraces an integrated and interfaith perspective, where other religious traditions reinforce the messages of Jesus and point us to God. Thank you, John Roger Barrie, for giving us this eternal and priceless gift!

–Anne Steinemann
December 2024

~~~~~~~~~~~~~

Anne Steinemann, PhD, has served as a university professor of civil and environmental engineering for three decades across the U.S. and Australia. Visit her website at www.drsteinemann.com.

Throughout her academic career, Dr. Steinemann has led and volunteered with Catholic ministries for the homeless, prisoners, student crisis counseling, defense of life, people with disabilities, refugees, and religious education. She has published two books of spiritual aphorisms: *Love is Like the Universe* and *Flying on the Wings of the Angels of Love*. Both books are available in a combined Special Edition, which is published by Sky Parlor Publications™, as is the separate edition of *Flying on the Wings of the Angels of Love*.

The Sacred Heart of Jesus statue
at Marymount High School, Los Angeles,
where it was located near Sunset Boulevard until 2020

FIRST AWAKENING:

A Spiritual Memoir

(adapted from *Dialogues With the Lord of Time*)

John Roger Barrie

Sky Parlor Publications™ · Nevada City, California

Library of Congress Control Number: 2024952566

ISBN: 979-8-9908834-3-7 (paperback)
ISBN: 979-8-9908834-5-1 (e-book)

First edition published December 2024.
Second printing, with minor corrections/edits, March 2025.

This book is an adapted and expanded chapter from *Dialogues With the Lord of Time,* Copyright © 2023 by John Roger Barrie.

Original watercolor artwork, *Sacred Heart of Jesus Statue,* hand painted by Lucie Mizutani and digitally enhanced by John Roger Barrie. Copyright © 2024 by John Roger Barrie. All Rights Reserved.

Unless otherwise noted, all photographs and images are by or owned by John Roger Barrie, Copyright © 2024 by John Roger Barrie.

Cover design and layout by Sky Parlor Publications™.

Sky Parlor Publications™ is a registered trademark in the United States of America.

Sky Parlor Publications™
P.O. Box 252
Nevada City, CA 95959
skyparlorpublications.com

*Dedicated with my warmest heartfelt love and gratitude
to the following:
–Nick J. Weber—empowering mentor,
–David Bowie and The Moody Blues—poets of the soul,
–Mark, Tim, Doug, and Jeffrey—loyal friends,
all of whose combined support
tremendously helped carry me through
this unparalleled autumn 1974 time period in my life.*

Also by John Roger Barrie

-Dialogues With the Lord of Time
A Novel of Spiritual Awakening

-The Deepest Silence and Other Essays
on Contemporary Spirituality

Contents

Preface

Fifty years ago, I underwent a profound spiritual experience that forever changed my life. The present book is a greatly expanded account of that experience, which I originally published in my spiritual novel, *Dialogues With the Lord of Time*, in early 2023.

While I recount several factors that collectively triggered this event, looking back I can see there were two principal events that actually portended it. The first was my car accident that happened around June 1974, when I overturned my VW van in West Los Angeles. Of all the places to come to a rest along legendary Sunset Boulevard, my car and I landed directly in front of a lifelike statue of Jesus, which was then located at the northwest corner of Marymount Place. In retrospect, this event appeared to foretell what would begin three short months later, as the statue of Jesus' outstretched arms seemingly scooped up and embraced a lost seventeen-year-old, who was then exploding with questions about his place in life and was very much receptive to the inspiration and guidance provided by Jesus' sublime, transformative messages.

The second event was my unforgettable eleven-day wilderness adventure in early August 1974, when I backpacked through California's jaw-dropping Sierra Nevada mountains. This left an indelible impression that changed my life and outlook.

The very heart and essence of my spiritual experience occurred during November 1974. I have been reliving this experience throughout the months of autumn 2024, and it seems fitting that most of this expanded account was assembled and written in November 2024. Further, as if a gift handed down from the cosmos to commemorate this mystical golden anniversary, the days of the week lined up in 2024 exactly as they originally took place in 1974.

A professor of religious studies once asked me why I called my spiritual experience the "First Awakening." My reply: "Hope springs eternal there will be a Second Awakening." Indeed, each unfolding of deepening spirituality in our lives develops more as a dynamic process of becoming rather than a static process of being, building and expanding on what came before, and incorporating the realizations from the past into the present, then carrying them into the future. The pivotal point for all such realizations in my life is fondly recalled in this memoir, which details a three-month spiritual unfolding that occurred in autumn 1974—my First Awakening.

John Roger Barrie
Nevada City, California
November 28, 2024

Acknowledgments

My deepest appreciation goes to the following individuals: Nick J. Weber for his lifelong inspirational influence; Anne Steinemann, PhD, for contributing her gracious and thoughtful *Appreciation*, which I am honored to have received, and which graces the front of my book; attorney Jonathan Kirsch, Esq; editor and author Rob Bignell for providing his expert editing recommendations for selected portions of the book; artist Lucie Mizutani for her skillful, realistic rendition of the *Sacred Heart of Jesus Statue*; and especially my wife Deborah Griffiths, whose unfailing support afforded me the dedicated time to prepare this manuscript for publication.

In addition, I extend my warmest gratitude to the following entities and persons for the courtesies they extended in granting their kind permission for me to use their copyrighted materials:

–Filmmaker Pete Bell and Yosemite National Park Ranger Shelton Johnson (for use of quotations by Yosemite National Park Ranger Shelton Johnson that first appeared in producer/director Pete Bell's 2011 documentary film, *High Sierra—A Journey on the John Muir Trail*).

–Marymount High School, Los Angeles (for use of their photograph of the Sacred Heart of Jesus statue; this photo has been cropped).

–Photographer John Reece (for use of his photographs: (1) *Looking North over Evolution Lake* (this photo has been cropped), Copyright © 2024 by John Reece; and (2) *Evolution Lake Looking South over Evolution Basin*, Copyright © 2021 by John Reece).

The two photos jointly titled "The Royal Lichtenstein Circus performance in October 1975 at the University of Memphis (featuring Nick J. Weber)" have been reproduced under license from the Special Collections Department, University of Memphis Libraries: (1) (Clown alone on stage) University Archives, Special Collections Department, University of Memphis Libraries; and (2) (Clown with students in stands) Memphis Press-Scimitar newspaper morgue, Special Collections Department, University of Memphis Libraries (this photo has been cropped). I am grateful to Michelle Duerr,

Digitization Archival Assistant with the Special Collections Department of the University of Memphis Libraries, for her help in facilitating my use of these photos.

Below are listed public domain or royalty-free sources for several images, some of which have been cropped or digitally enhanced.

–"Title page from first edition of Henry David Thoreau's *Walden* (1854)" (Public domain, via Wikimedia Commons).

–"Man Fire Flame Burning" (uploaded by user *andsproject*, via Pixabay).

–"Cross Clip Art" (uploaded by user *Ocal*, via Clker.com).

–"Students watch circus performers at the student union—Tallahassee, Florida" (by Deborah Thomas, Florida State University, March 13, 1985, PDM 1.0).

–"Bronze statue of Peter Pan located in Kensington Gardens, London" (uploaded by user *Sebjarod*, Public domain, via Wikimedia Commons).

All color photos have been desaturated for the print edition of this book. My own photos and images have been digitally enhanced and/or modified for appearance, size, and/or content.

Note: The thoughts and opinions expressed in this book are solely those of the author and do not necessarily reflect the views, neither do they constitute endorsements, either express or implied, of those entities and persons listed in this Acknowledgements section.

Introduction

I had repeatedly edited the final 11,044-word version of the chapter "A Spiritual Memoir" from my spiritual novel *Dialogues With the Lord of Time*, for length and content. There is no question that this chapter was essential to the plot; it provided an indispensable point of reference around which hung the underlying running *leitmotif* of the entire narrative. But, while essential, I had to ensure this chapter would not detract from the novel's *über* theme, which consisted of dialogues and teachings by the main character, Father Christopher, and his influence and transforming impact on the lives of those who studied with him.

In my Author's Note for *Dialogues*, I used carefully chosen words to characterize the book as "inspired by my own real-life experiences, but I have fictionalized many accounts and have written [the book] as a work of fiction in its entirety. All characters and their identifying characteristics, including the first-person narrator and the character called Father Christopher, are fictional or have been fictionalized, in whole or in part. Any similarities between the fictional and fictionalized characters in my book and real persons are strictly coincidental." This was a necessary legal disclaimer, but the wording leaves the door open as to which exactly are the "real-life experiences" and which are the "many accounts" that have been "fictionalized." And, to what extent, "in whole or in part," have the characters been fictionalized. One percent? Ninety-nine percent?

The one chapter from *Dialogues* that fully recounts an entirely real-life experience is "A Spiritual Memoir," except for references to the narrative from *Dialogues* at the very beginning and very end of this chapter. [March 2025 update: In addition, I have corrected a two-sentence passage about "grasses" and "birches" in new printings of both the present book and *Dialogues* after having carefully consulted my earliest writing of this recollection from Dec. 7, 1985, and determining this reference was meant to be used analogously, not nonfictionally as it previously had been characterized. The corrected passage now reflects this analogous description.] The "Spiritual Memoir" chapter is also where the "first-person narrator" is the actually myself, John Roger Barrie. But this chapter was subjected to several rounds of drastic edits I made prior to publication so it would flow quickly and not impede the overall storyline of the book.

For the present standalone edition of this chapter, which is published during the fiftieth anniversary of this transformative event in my life, I have reincorporated many sections that were edited out or simply unused in the original, mostly consisting of descriptive footnotes and supplemental material. At the time, I deemed some of this additional material too esoteric or too unusual to include in *Dialogues With the Lord of Time*. However, I am including the vast majority of this heretofore omitted, unpublished material in this edition, while at the same time retaining a few fictional elements, which I have listed in the Author's Note immediately below. In addition, I have amended the existing text with further recollections that expand on many sections in greater detail, and I've added three appendices. The resultant text is more than 2.75 times the size of the original chapter in *Dialogues*, excluding the new Preface and Introduction I've included in this edition. Finally, I have included several scans from my actual late 1974 to early 1975 journals, some of which contain minor spelling errors.

While there has been a disconcerting movement afoot in contemporary religious studies to discount, even belittle, mystical experience, there has been a much-needed countermovement that seeks once again to legitimize it. My hope in expanding this account of a seventeen-year-old's inner spiritual journey is to add another narrative, however minor, to the corpus of literature on the topic.

–John Roger Barrie

Author's Note: The names of persons in the present edition are fictional, except for the following: Anne Steinemann PhD; the individuals whom I have gratefully recognized in the Acknowledgments section; the semi-anonymized "John B" portion of the *Deficiency Report* image (where another name has been fully redacted); Nick J. Weber, whom I mention in the narrative; and the actual names of real persons that are mentioned incidentally in the narrative and notes. No sponsorship by or affiliation with the owners of trademarks that are mentioned in passing is claimed or suggested.

Whenever "he" or "she," "him" or "her," "his" or "hers," or "himself" or "herself" are used as nonspecific pronouns, such usage is intended in a gender-neutral sense.

First Awakening

IT WAS OCTOBER 1991. [Note: In these opening three paragraphs, I have retained the existing fictional narrative from my novel *Dialogues With the Lord of Time*, although my conversation with Patrick below was factual.] Autumn is my favorite time of year. I deeply resonate with each change of season, and I become especially indrawn and introspective during the fall months. I had been increasing the length of my meditations, and many times my mind would effortlessly cease to function and become absorbed in a deep spiritual current. Yet, this was causing me conflict. On the one hand, I had a necessary involvement with the world. But on the other hand, I wanted to sever all worldly ties and dive wholly into my spiritual practices. I could not seem to integrate the two worlds, which at times seemed poles apart.

A high-school friend, Patrick, and I once analyzed what separated Jesus, Gandhi, Martin Luther King Jr., and certain other iconoclastic notables from the crowd. "They never compromised," he observed. That insight has stayed with me through the years. I, too, had aspired to be in a position where someday I would not have to compromise. On that day, I would be able to live my spiritual vision without watering it down. But in October 1991, I felt haunted by the recurring thought that I had abandoned my spiritual roots. I'd adopted the customs and views of the society in which I lived. I'd focused on making money and, while I was satisfied with my then-current level of earnings, I'd also chosen to live a life of voluntary simplicity as enjoined by Thoreau.[1] Yet, *all this* at the expense of nourishing my soul? At times I felt lost.

I drove from my apartment and headed north toward Father Christopher's cabin. I had spoken with Heather and told her that I planned to camp out at MacKerricher State Park rather than stay with her. Gail and I were drifting apart, and I didn't want to fuel the estrangement. Besides, I needed to be alone. I needed to unearth something inside of me that had been buried since my life-altering spiritual experience of 1974, my self-described First Awakening.

~~~~~~~~~~~~~

This was the pivotal, defining event in my life, lasting from early September through mid-December 1974. For slightly more than three months, the portals of heaven opened up. I consider all the incidents in my life as leading up and referring back to this one central experience. Even now, its living presence occasionally engulfs me. It only needs the proper setting to resurface.

A number of factors influenced and presaged this event. Beginning in my mid-teens, I saw how most of humankind had enshrouded itself in an artificial, contrived reality that is completely cut off from nature and the spiritual realm. I felt that people were programmed from childhood into accepting a worldview based on materialistic values. They embraced conventions, such as time and language, which only reinforced their conditioning. They created cities to perpetuate their artificial environment. I clearly believed that humans were in the grip of a mass, illusive lie. This line of thinking persisted and became my predominant mindset through my late teens and early twenties; it enlivened and inspired me. It shaped the very essence of my view of life.

During this formative period, I had serendipitously developed my philosophical belief system based on my limited life experience and my own observations. For the most part, it was unspoiled by formal education and, except for less than a handful of admired writers, it was largely unaffected by the thoughts of others. I had encountered the writings of those whom I considered the three classic nineteenth-century nonpolitician American philosophers—Emerson, Thoreau, and Muir,[2] all of whom exerted a significant influence on me—together with a smattering of Eastern thinkers, but none too influential.[3]

Title page from first edition of Henry David Thoreau's *Walden* (1854)

My mind was not filled with rigid preconceptions or dogmatic beliefs. I was open, unspecialized, raw. I intentionally avoided learning different intellectual and technical details about things, such as the scientific names of trees. I felt this would dilute and color my direct interaction with and immediate experience of these objects. I believed that outside knowledge only tainted people's minds with potential bias, and it predisposed them to accept information passively, unquestioningly, rather than actively and consciously acquiring it. Thus, I aspired to learn and absorb knowledge on my own wherever possible and not through books or by way of other people's accounts, which I generally shunned, as I distrusted so-called experts. I felt that too much reading provided a person with secondhand analytical information, which tended to overshadow a more direct, experiential mode of learning. I sought firsthand knowledge, free from intermediaries and extrinsic interpretations. In short, I needed to find out things for myself. As my mother occasionally told me during my childhood, coincidentally citing Thoreau, "You march to the beat of a different drummer." I further believed that all people could—and should, ideally—similarly acquire knowledge on their own with minimal outside instruction. I felt this learn-it-yourself method of educating oneself was an innate ability that remained dormant within every individual.

Unquenchable Fire

When I began my senior year at my all-boys high school, there were several events that molded my outlook. First, I had recently under-taken an unforgettable wilderness adventure. I leisurely hiked the 55-mile North Lake to South Lake loop trail in the Eastern High Sierra when backpacking with a friend, Kevin, from August 3 to 13, 1974. This left an indelible impression on my young, sensitive mind. The all-enveloping presence of nature swallowed me up and drained me of human perspectives. I vividly recall losing all sense of distance and, even more important, of time. For eleven priceless days, I lived on na-ture's terms, completely removed from the endless concrete and droning roar of Lost Angeles, as I then called the unforgiving city.

This adventure affected me so intensely that it transformed me; my soul was transported from this very world. I had never been so thoroughly wonderstruck in all my life. I endlessly marveled at the numerous jaw-dropping spectacles of nature I encountered in this sublime high-country mountain pavilion where I traversed and camped. I wrote about this outing in early 1979: "It took three or four days to divest me of myself. The magic then descended full force. The Sierra began engulfing me." This mood swept me up, and I couldn't leave it behind when I left the mountains. "I clung to it like a jeweled treasure chest—it revived me, rekindled me. I became fully alive with it." I again wrote in 1985: "Man's creations paled into tripe. I touched God. I lived free. I [became] vibrantly and dangerously alive, scintillating with utter madness."

Looking North over Evolution Lake (cropped)

As Yosemite National Park Ranger Shelton Johnson commented in 2011, very much echoing the spirit of John Muir, "I think the best way to travel these places is with a sense of reverence, that it's an honor to be in this kind of environment, and this is a sacred place and to treat it as a sacred place. You know, when people walk into a church, their voices before they walk in may be loud and they may be just kind of blustery and all of that. As soon as they walk in, there's this hush and there's this calm; there's this stillness that takes over you. Even if it's a church that's not of your faith. So, I think it's the same thing when you enter a trail into the wilderness—there should be a sense of reverence, of spiritual connection. It's just a place where the divine is manifest on earth."[4]

Second, coupled with my awestruck experience of nature, I was confronted with the reality of having to go to college, learn a vocation, and become part of the establishment. I shuddered at the thought of losing my philosophical orientation, to say nothing of losing my close friends, and most of all, leaving my sacred personal world. I had watched others capitulate to the system. When they did, the luster disappeared from their eyes and the spark became extinguished in their soul. As I wrote on September 13, 1974, I did not want to "let my friends become entangled in the cobweb of society." Neither did I want the same fate to befall me. I did not want the world to win. I would not succumb to the pressure of being fashioned into someone else's idea of who I should be. Neither could I do something for a living that I loathed by virtue of slaving away at some mindless, unrewarding job that would define my role in society.[5] I would not live as a robotized zombie.

Admittedly, I was not exactly establishment material. In the fall of that year, in front of our high-school chapel, my friend Ed asked me what I wanted to do in life. I replied, "Wander from town to town and spread joy to all people, telling them all about love." While my youthful idealism was admirable, it most likely would not have put bread on my table. I also dreamt of living alone in a small house or cabin in the Sierra Nevada mountain range, which also would not quite be considered a formula for worldly success. My unambitious goals were not those expected of a typical college-bound student, and they would not have particularly endeared me to any college-admissions board. The truth is that I refused to live a life I felt was totally foreign to me. Instead of adapting and quietly conforming to the average American way of life, which I viewed as conceding to the commonplace status quo, I desperately wanted to escape.

On September 28 of that momentous year, I penned a nature poem for a class assignment that encapsulated my longing for liberation (with edits):

> Mystic meadow madness: compassionate music.
> Above me, mountain king beckons
> Below, guardian trees embrace waning stream.
> Like the sun endlessly circling
> Or the night sky in motion,
> I will travel all roads
> Never to bemoan the dead ends
> Until I am led
> To the path with no chains.

Third, a sobering event at my Catholic high school profoundly affected me. When driving out of the school parking lot onto the adjacent street one afternoon in early September, I saw a friend, Marty, in the car behind me. True to our teenage horseplay, I raised my right hand and jokingly saluted him with the *digitus impudicus*, not once but two or three times, goading him on, fully expecting him playfully to reciprocate. But there was no response. When I looked more closely in my rearview mirror, I realized that he was actually a *she*, and she was fuming mad. She drove straight around the corner and parked in front of the administration office, then marched herself inside. And I, aghast and embarrassed at my horrible mistake, sheepishly followed her. Inconsolable and raving, this high-school mother let everyone within earshot know the debased nature of my crime, especially—alas—the principal. My repeated apologies did nothing to assuage her unrelenting tirade.

Crestfallen, I, too, met with the Jesuit principal minutes later, who no doubt could see my face oozing remorse, along with abject, palpable fear as to my fate. I expected him to sentence me to weeks of detention—the dreaded afterschool incarceration known as *jug*,[6] wherein many a recalcitrant soul was forced to recite obscure Latin texts, or worse, he could have directed me to memorize stanzas by Milton.[7] Or he could have suspended me, which was well within his purview, for my regrettable and unintended offending behavior.

But he simply said, "Always remember, actions speak louder than words."

"Actions speak louder than words." This dictum proved far more powerful than any punishment. In that moment of utter receptivity, those words sank to the core of my being, so much so that they became a lifelong theme, an ideal worthy of emulation. The principal's profound utterance, stemming from compassion and insight, deeply planted in me a seed that radically altered my attitude. From that instant on, and especially during this autumn 1974 time period, I realized I could not compartmentalize my life. Thoughts, intentions, words, deeds—all must be brought into alignment so they match without discord. A person cannot preach one thing and practice another. One must root out all double standards within oneself. Consequently, after this incident and for the remainder of my First

Awakening, I purposefully avoided talking much about myself. My actions became my primary speech.

Fourth, and lastly, three classes in my senior year deeply affected me. I had written on January 29, 1975, "School is too slow a pace for me. I catch on things much faster than other people have judged me as doing." Despite my optimistic self-assessment and my predilection to acquire knowledge on my own, the skillful teachers who taught these courses gently imbued me with understandings that I could not have gained myself. Responding in kind to the challenges they posed that lay before me, I dove headlong to find meaning in these classes.

The first class consisted of a course that examined morality and values, and what I learned turned me inside out. The young lay instructor adeptly goaded us to think about life, about the deeper meaning of events, about ourselves, and how all these issues intersected.

The second class was theology, based on the practical application of New Testament teachings. The ordained teacher imparted to us his impassioned sense of helping the poor and the marginalized. I once attended the Jail Run program, one of the ministries he oversaw. He focused on alleviating hunger, which greatly influenced me. This eye-opening introduction to hands-on spirituality made me painfully aware of the plight of poor people. At times, I felt more concern for them than for myself. Once during this time, I fasted for two days—which was significant for me in light of my fast metabolism—so that I could experience the same sensation of hunger they felt. While I never participated in the class's soup-kitchen outreach program, I occasionally donated my extra lunch money to the cause. I began to identify with those who struggled in life, and my concern evoked feelings of compassion within me. I felt their pain on a visceral level, and this identification tremendously stirred me and occasionally caused me to weep at their plight. It distressed me that so few people cared about their predicament or tried to change their lot in life.

My exposure to these newly uncovered psychological and social issues set into motion inner awakenings that were far more than spiritual. I went through a crash course in political, societal, and environmental realizations. Without fully understanding the system, I knew it was wrong by the effects it produced—inequality and injustice, mistreatment and exploitation of many, a lopsided social structure, unfair economic allotments, widespread pollution, and ecological imbalances. The effects of my high-school courses fermented inside me and thus served to kindle a larger awareness in me. This onrush of social issues triggered in me a new depth of understanding along with a strong inner protest of and contempt for "the system." I began to deeply distrust and abhor the establishment.

The third class I took was photography. For my homework assignments, I would snap pictures of my favorite haunts: the spectacular view from the seaside cliffs high on the Palos Verdes peninsula overlooking the rippling blue, whitecap-tinted Pacific Ocean; Temescal Canyon and the surrounding lush Pacific Palisades environs; Brooktree Road and the adjoining magical streets that wend around Rustic Creek and Rustic Canyon Recreation Center in verdant Santa Monica Canyon; the sheltered enclaves in the Crestwood Hills neighborhood adjacent to North Kenter and Hanley avenues along the scenic Brentwood highlands; several expansive vista points off iconic, sinuous Mulholland Drive between Stone Canyon Road and fabled Laurel Canyon Boulevard; the stately residential areas east of UCLA and nearby Holmby Park; the winding hillside roads north of Sunset Boulevard between Beverly Glen Boulevard and Coldwater Canyon Drive that snake around lavish mansions and hidden bungalows; and the then-secluded Franklin Canyon Reservoir greenbelts.

This class made me conscious of how to look at the world around me. The lay teacher gave us some valuable technical pointers. I would no longer take for granted the interplay between shadow and light, or color. I became acutely aware of the vibrant Impressionist-like multicolored hues that constantly surround us, if we only paid attention. When snapping a photo, I would intuitively learn to sight the best angles to optimally frame an object, and I'd instinctively account for depth of field when juxtaposing foreground and background elements. However, I wasn't just taking pictures. During my First Awakening, my camera became a lens looking not into the outer world but into my soul. Photography turned into a spiritual exercise that enabled me to capture externally what my soul was perceiving internally. Thus, I viewed the world from an entirely new perspective, and my newly discovered capacity to look at things from a different vantage point carried over into my daily life.

Hence, the amalgam of my unconventional, individualist mind-set and my unorthodox worldview; my reluctance to conform to establishment norms; my entrenched resistance to becoming a collegebound functionary; my lingering, overpoweringly moving impression of nature during my Sierra Nevada backpacking trip; my genuine remorse at having inadvertently offended someone; my effort to rid myself of hypocrisy; my ability to see the world in a new light; and my newfound cognizance of macro issues, including identifying with and feeling sympathy for the poor, reached a fever pitch in me. These circumstances upended my world. Part of me refused to move forward, to "grow up," to attend college, to waste away in a system devoid of meaning. I could have cared less about career, money, family, responsibility, participation, and involvement—all of which I shunned. I just wanted to remain in a playful, contented state and retain my childhood freedoms, without a care in the world.

The combined influences of these events, coupled with my misgivings and deeply troubled feelings when starting my senior year and what to do after school ended, catalyzed me by squeezing my soul into one all-encompassing scream, an inner cry, which insistently implored: *I want out!* I madly sought refuge from the imprisonment of home, family, school, society, and self. I became seized with questioning, inquisitiveness, and a sense of reckless abandon, caring not for the morrow or any conventional course of action. And so, this fervor, this unquenchable fire, rapidly grew within me.

a Man, as I know from personal experience, ~~too~~ has to ask questions in order To be delivered from the ~~the~~ finite to the infinite. If a man does not ask questions, he (may) tend to, as "they" say, "settle in his ways," then, as I see it that will be his own ~~def~~ definition version of heaven & hell good & evil in an ultimate sense. The (choise) bad is the man's own to step out of his own limits his own boundaries

"[A] man, as I know from personal experience, has to ask questions in order to be delivered from the finite to the infinite."

Scan of original approx. December 1, 1974, holographic writing

No Use for This Body

I had been an average teen growing up in the early 1970s. I was raised in an upper-middle-class home. My father was Catholic, my mother Episcopalian. While I was brought up in the Catholic tradition, I was not overtly religious insofar as I did not regularly attend church. My activities and interests consisted of normal, ordinary teen fare. I underwent typical adolescent adventures—and certainly my share of misadventures when learning about life. While generally well behaved, I sporadically displayed an obstreperous "little hellion" component to my character during my grammar school and early high-school years, which I thankfully outgrew. Thus, I neither presented myself nor thought of myself as pious, and I sincerely doubt that anyone would have singled me out as particularly spiritual or devout.

But the aggregate effect of the combined events listed in the previous chapter when beginning my senior year in early September 1974 impinged on the deepest levels of my being and threw my personal life into utter disarray. My whole mindset changed. My priorities shifted. This inner crisis had shaken my world and turned it upside down. But instead of ignoring these events and their impact on me, I became utterly receptive to them. I was keenly attuned to the disruptive change that was in the air and burrowing through me, and I embraced it. I was acutely seeking answers to the sudden dilemmas that now affected me, and this inner yearning is precisely what prompted me to turn to God. My behavior markedly began to change.

The cherubic-looking boy at his First Holy Communion on May 9, 1965. But wait—on closer look, what's that shiner under his left eye? My mother, wearing a mink stole, is seen in the background.

In the evening hours, I would grab our family Bible located on the closet shelf outside my bedroom door. Then I'd shut myself in my room and seal out all light by drawing the shades and blocking the bottom of my door until all cracks of light were covered and the room was pitch dark, except for the light given off by my bedside floor lamp.[8] Then, sitting on the side of my bed, I would randomly open and flip through the pages of my Bible until my eyes fell on a seemingly intended passage, often a reflective or inspirational verse from Psalms, Proverbs, or one of the books of the New Testament. Of course, I always loved reading my favorite sections—Matthew Chapter 6 and John 14–15, along with various verses from Psalms and Proverbs. Afterward, I would diligently attempt to practice whatever biblical passage I had read. Simply recalling these passages provided spiritual solace during the daytime hours.

At first, my biblical readings were relatively shallow; I would take in their surface message. But later, they became deeper, more profound. I was emotionally engaged, which helped me to absorb the teaching. Regardless of what passage I read, I felt the message was specifically intended for me, that it was *my* message, and reverberations of its truth shuddered throughout the deepest recesses of my soul. I'd fix my attention on that one passage alone, as if nothing else existed, learning whatever lesson it offered, absorbing the essence of its meaning until it alone resonated inside me.[9] Utilizing an intense degree of undisturbable concentration, I merged with my reading—*became* the teaching, as my receptive mind was entirely calm and focused. Thus, I prayed the Bible slowly, word by word, and each idea came alive in my heart.

My family Bible, which I keep near me to this day

15

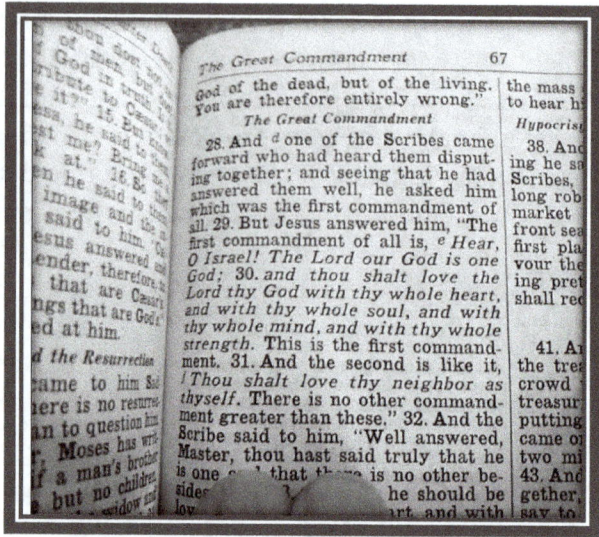

Page from my family Bible

I would then shed my clothing, turn off my bedside light and, amid the piercing darkness that enveloped me, I'd lie face up on my bed, using no pillow, with my open Bible held face down on my chest, over my heart. I felt repugnance at the very thought of any encumbrances, which prompted me to remove my clothing. I'd slightly prop up my feet[10] and, remaining as motionless as possible, I would systematically focus my attention on each body part from toes to head as I repeatedly commanded my legs, arms, torso, neck, and head to *relax* until they were rendered limp and devoid of all tension. My technique drained each body part of all sensation, of all autonomous reactions. I later learned my method paralleled the practice of *pratyahara*, "turning the mind inward," from Patanjali's eight-limbed yoga system, whereby *prana* or energy is withdrawn from the senses and the external world, which is a form of sense deprivation that is achieved mentally. This practice caused me to be utterly relaxed; my body was lying still like a corpse. I numbed my mind to any physical sensation.[11] I would not allow so much as a muscular twitch or an itching sensation[12] to disturb my ultra-relaxed, comalike state, and I resisted normal bodily processes such as urges to change position or to swallow. Then, I would immerse myself in what I later learned was meditation, although at the time I had no idea what this was called.

16

As I intuitively strove for an undiluted spiritual experience, I actively evicted all thoughts floating through my head. I forced my mind to cease functioning. I thoroughly quelled my rational mind by stopping every type of mental activity. More than anything, I sought to blot out all trace of self. I mustered up all my strength to extinguish my sense of "I-ness" completely. I tried to annihilate all separateness, all individuality.

Often in combination with my Bible-reading routine, I would similarly lie on my bed and play sides of a select few of my favorite albums, most frequently the transcendent *To Our Children's Children's Children* and the equally transcendent *Every Good Boy Deserves Favour*, both by the Moody Blues; and the three largely introspective, empowering early RCA releases by David Bowie—*Space Oddity, The Man Who Sold The World*, and *Hunky Dory*. I possessed a fairly decent stereo system for a high-school teen: Marantz 2220 receiver, Dual turntable with Shure cartridge, and University Stereo's modest in-house two-way bookshelf speakers.

The Moody Blues had long made an impression. I clearly remember riding an escalator in a shopping mall and listening to "Tuesday Afternoon" as it was softly broadcast on the P.A. system when accompanying my paternal grandmother on an errand while visiting our grandparents in Evanston, Illinois during the summer of 1968. My friend Rob and I repeatedly played *Children's Children* in late 1969 and 1970. I was temporarily living with my father when I acquired *Every Good Boy*; I recall playing it on a small portable record player and being mesmerized by the opening sequence of exotic sounds and voices on the first track, "Procession."

Song lyrics moved me emotionally and spiritually, exerting a profound effect. In my journal writings from 1974 and 1975, I had written out and cited a number of influential lyrics, including "I Am a Rock" by Simon and Garfunkel, "My Song" by Mike Pinder of the Moody Blues, as well as lines by Mike's bandmates Justin Hayward and John Lodge, along with lyrics by Cat Stevens, Joni Mitchell, Graham Nash, Stephen Stills, Ian Anderson, and songs by David Bowie.

My then circle of friends introduced me to Bowie around 1972. While we never embraced the Bowie glam-rock attire or gender-bending lifestyle, we nonetheless were collective Bowie fanatics, and we repeatedly played his albums. I recall the day when Kelly, an older friend, gave me money and asked me to purchase *Hunky Dory* for him; he described the cover as Bowie holding his head, overflowing with long, golden-hued hair, gazing skyward. We'd play *Space Oddity* and *The Man Who Sold The World* as well, then *Ziggy Stardust* and *Aladin Sane* as time wore on. Bowie's inventive musical fluidity, innovative ear-candy arrangements, impeccable musicianship, sparkling studio production, and the topics he addressed all hugely appealed and spoke to me on the deepest level. His occasional nonsensical lyrics didn't matter; he sang with conviction, and I was completely attuned to his vocal wavelength, the timbre of his intonations, and his unique pronunciation and inflections. I related to him as I did no other artist during this time in my life, save of course the Moody Blues. I'd memorize songs from my prized David Bowie songbook or teach myself any number of Bowie songs on guitar and piano, then sing and play my heart out.

The Bowie songs on *Space Oddity* that particularly affected me were "Space Oddity," "Cygnet Committee," "Letter to Hermoine," "Janine," the hauntingly evocative "An Occasional Dream," and particularly "Wild Eyed Boy from Freecloud," with its themes of alienation, seeming defeat, then triumph. From *The Man Who Sold the World*, I especially resonated with "The Width of a Circle" (although I could not relate to the allusive sexual imagery in part two of the song) and "All the Madmen," then "After All," "Saviour Machine," "The Man Who Sold the World," and "The Supermen." The songs with which I most identified on *Hunky Dory* were "Changes," "Oh! You Pretty Things," "Life on Mars?," especially "Quicksand" and "Fill Your Heart," and "Bewlay Brothers." However, all of Bowie's songs, including ones not listed above—"God Knows I'm Good," "Kooks," "Andy Warhol," "Song for Bob Dylan," played interiorly on the turntable of my heart.

I had arranged the speakers in my room on either side of my bed to achieve perfect stereo balance, and I would lie perfectly still in the middle of my bed—the sweet spot—and focus intensely on the music until my mind attained a state of deep concentration. I would force all stray thoughts to stop. In so doing, I heard each lyric and musical note as if for the first time, as my once busy mind was emptied of all thoughts and would no longer interfere with my direct perception of the music. My mind was thus concentrated to the utmost degree, and

I became totally oblivious to all else. I fused and *became* one with the music to which I was listening, as I felt no lingering division between the music and my sense of self. Once I transcended my awareness of duality, I experienced only oneness with no separate existence. This unitive sensation began lingering with me into activity.

Unbeknown to me, I was using music as a means to meditate and as a focal point to still my mind. Thus, while I was deeply attuned to the messages and music of both Bowie and the Moodies, it wasn't these artists in themselves that catalyzed my meditations; it was what awakened in me due to my listening to them with utter mental focus. Sometimes it took me longer to calm my mind than other times, but typically I achieved a profoundly deep state of unruffled concentration after listening to one or at most two sides of an album. Thus, my main spiritual practice was mind control, which was conjoined with devotion, although I did not label them as such.

In my novel, I wrote that "I would also briefly perform vigorous exercise before lying down to meditate ..." That specific vigorous exercise consisted of my version of dancing. While playing mostly Bowie songs or even songs by The Moodies, I would often dance along to the music, acting out and *becoming* the lyrics of each song until I lost myself entirely. Then I would lie down to meditate. This routine had the effect of releasing any surplus bodily tension, which induced a state of physical calmness that proved conducive to meditation. By strongly emotionally identifying with a given song, I consolidated my wandering mind and intensified my focus, which helped propel me into deep meditation. I occasionally sang along with these songs, which helped me to merge with them until I felt no sensation of duality. Later on, during November and onward, I slackened off on my cathartic dance routine, as its purpose had been accomplished insofar as I had integrated its effects into my consciousness.

These practices allowed my inner being to enter a timeless realm wherein my ability to distinguish outer from inner, object from subject, and music from listener, had vanished. My sense of self-consciousness dissolved, and I became inwardly rapt in deep meditation. I soon craved this loss of self more than anything.

As I had essentially no one with whom I could share my experiences, I turned to the one friend to whom I had turned during previous times of crisis in my life, my one true friend who never deserted me, even though I typically, and shamefully, left him when my adverse circumstances improved. My eternal friend whose words I found in our family Bible—my friend Jesus, with whom I reacquainted myself. Jesus' teachings came alive in me. I began to view him as the anchor and foundation of my life.

In addition to meditating, I prayed to God from the deepest level of my being, calling out for guidance and direction. I would kneel next to my bed and send forth spontaneous, heartfelt outpourings directly from my soul to God. I felt an unimaginable longing to immerse myself in the infinite expanse of God. When praying, I envisioned God as a formless, omnipresent, yet very much living and palpable entity. I felt especially safe, knowing that God was present and on my side. However, praying to Jesus was much easier because I would picture him as he is commonly portrayed in popular images.

Once I made the sign of the Cross, I established a deep connection with God. What followed was a focused intensity and outpouring of raw emotion. When I conversed with God, streams of tears often spontaneously gushed forth. I engaged in the most heartfelt, unprompted, unplanned, totally absorbed exchanges with my God. I would plead for guidance, forgiveness, and mercy. My soul was laid bare, stripped of all pretentions. There, utterly vulnerable, I sought divine grace. "Jesus, forgive me!" "Lord, help me!"

I would say the Our Father, Hail Mary, and Glory Be, essentially praying my adapted version of the Rosary. When reciting the Lord's Prayer, I would typically picture each part and repeat it slowly, deliberately, one syllable at a time, until each word became animated in my heart. I clearly visualized and imbued each phrase with meaning as I worked my way through the prayer. "Give us our daily bread" included all humanity. I felt "Forgive us our trespasses" at a visceral level, which helped me to cultivate humility. "We forgive those who trespass against us," and by so doing, the pain of another's stinging words or thoughtless actions would mitigate. "Lead us not into temptation," but rather hold us in Your loving arms. God is here, present now; God consoles. All is resolved in God. Then I made the sign of the Cross, signaling the end of my prayer, and these most intense, communications with God now came to an end until my next session.

My frequent tearful Godward entreaties washed away the darkness concealing my spirit. My soul was laid bare, stripped of all pretentions. I invoked the living presence of God through the sheer force of my prayers—the vague became tangible; the invisible, known; the unseen, powerfully felt. My prayers drew me outside of myself and, at the same time, drew God closer to me. When I prayed, every cell of my being was on fire. This had the effect of eroding layer upon layer of the encrusted sheaths of worldliness that had covered my soul.

I started to follow a very basic path, as clearly outlined in my New Testament readings:

What is my purpose in life?
  "Seek first the kingdom of God."[13]
What is God?
  "God is Spirit."[14] "God is love."[15]
Where can I find God?
  "The kingdom of God is within you."[16]
How can I know God?
  "Love the Lord your God with all your heart, with all your soul, with all your mind, and with all your strength" and "Love your neighbor as yourself."[17]
But what of other concerns?
  "Where your treasure is, there your heart will be also."[18] "You cannot love both God and mammon."[19]
What, then, must I do?
  "Whoever hears these words of mine and puts them into practice is like a wise man who builds his house upon a rock."[20] "Come, follow me."[21]

It was so simple what I was to do, and I proceeded to do it, forcefully throwing off all hindrances that would prevent me from following and scrupulously applying these life-transforming teachings of Jesus and his direct disciples. This round-the-clock effort required marshaling all my energies so I could attend to this one goal.

Night after night, I continued my secret activity. When I arrived home from school, I couldn't wait to dive back into my spiritual practices. My new inner world captivated me far more than the outer world, and I eagerly and passionately resumed my newly established routines. My room became my private shelter; its shrouding darkness provided a sanctuary to my soul, which was emerging as if from a long slumber. I had found my refuge, my escape. While the world slept, I remained vibrantly awake and fully attentive during the benevolent nighttime hours, praying for release from my worldly fetters. When I finally fell asleep, I drifted off quickly and slept soundly. I consciously slept on my back. If I awoke later in the night, I'd often repeat my routine of Bible reading, prayer, and meditation. I would sometimes begin my prayers at night and, upon waking, finish the same prayer the next morning. I never allowed myself to relax or slacken my efforts. I thrust myself into my new routines with the full force of my being, which I eagerly pursued at all costs.

For the first several weeks, I inexplicably suffered from intense daytime sleepiness. I complained about this to a close friend, Mark. I felt overwhelmingly tired all the time, yet I forced myself to work through this strange malady. I believed my fatigue was a demonic temptation of sorts. Then one day, it came to an end. My unrelenting fervent intensity of purpose and undeterred determination had propelled me through this difficult period and allowed me to overcome it. Around one week after I complained to him, Mark asked me about my sleepiness; I told him it had passed. After this sleepy period, I felt well rested all the time. Sleep itself had essentially become irrelevant. I felt that food, clothing, even my body—anything and everything that would drag my mind down to material existence—was a superfluous encumbrance. I readily jettisoned anything that would interfere in the slightest with my ability to maintain the spiritual reality that was discernably growing within me.

In my spiritual novel *Dialogues With the Lord of Time*, the main character Father Christopher explains the phenomenon of sleepiness. "When you meditate, you are swimming against the evolutionary tide. The tendency of the mind is to focus outwardly. Just as a child is mesmerized when playing with its toys, the mind similarly craves to be entertained and occupied by an incessant stream of thoughts, emotions, and external objects. When you meditate you reverse this outward tendency, which goes against the mind's natural inclination. This can result in fatigue or sleepiness, especially at the beginning of one's spiritual quest, because it takes

22

a great deal of energy first to turn your mind inward, then to concentrate it until it becomes completely devoid of thoughts."

All the while, my external world was crumbling apart. My high school work suffered; in fact, I was so completely seized by my all-consuming, round-the-clock craving for freedom that I neglected to do most homework. I was failing in all my classes, with "D" to "F" averages, which were radically departures from my grade averages in past semesters.[22] But I simply didn't care, as evidenced by the nonchalant note I wrote on one of my January 14, 1975 homework assignments: "Despite the grade you give me, whether it be "A" or "F," [it] won't matter to me …"

I'd also proffer answers in classes that weren't exactly what the instructors were seeking. For example, one teacher requested our solutions to the problem of how to curb widespread noxious automotive exhaust fumes. My response, "Don't drive cars," ignited a contagion of similar replies from other students afire with their own epiphanies. "Yeah, just stop driving!" However, I wasn't being snarky, just practical. In January 1975, I had drafted plans for an electric car, as seen in the images below. I even visited a battery supply shop, sizing up my plans. But this idea was not to reach fruition, as I truly lacked worldly ambition and the real-world wherewithal to implement such ideas.

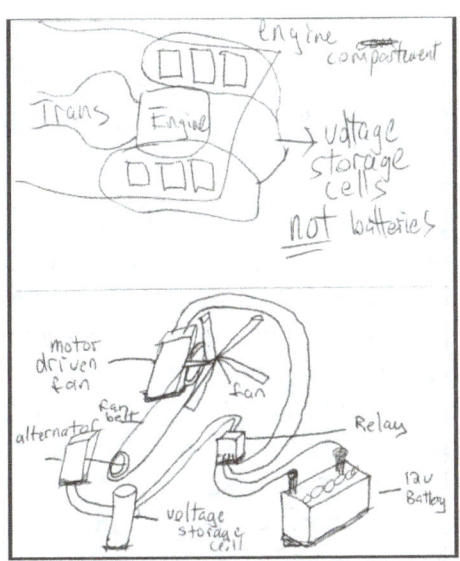

My early 1975 plans for an all-electric vehicle to help rid the world of smog. Copyright © 2024 by John Roger Barrie.

I was called in for a meeting by the principal, who warned me about my failing grades. At my request, he gave me another chance. I did make some effort, but only half-heartedly, and I soon abandoned all attempts to rectify my sinking academic standing.

PARENT'S COPY		

STUDENT'S NAME *John B*

DEFICIENCY REPORT

DATE *Jan 7 1975*

CLASS *SR*

TEACHER

SUBJECT *20th Cent History*

ADVISER

NOTICE TO PARENTS

1. The student is presently in academic difficulty in this subject, and consequently there is the danger of failure.
2. It is necessary that the cause(s) of this deficiency be understood and the recommendation(s) be followed.
3. Make certain that you are familiar with the school's grading system and the suggested amount of homework expected in the subject each night.

CAUSE(S) FOR DEFICIENCY:

ABILITY	ATTITUDE	PERFORMANCE
☐ POOR APTITUDE IN SUBJECT	☑ POOR ATTENDANCE/LATENESS.	☑ POOR TEST SCORES.
☐ INADEQUATE FOUNDATION IN SUBJECT.	☑ INADEQUATE PREPARATION FOR CLASS.	☑ INADEQUATE WRITTEN HOMEWORK OR NOTES.
☑ LACK OF EFFECTIVE MOTIVATION.	☑ LACK OF SERIOUS APPROACH TO STUDIES.	☑ LACK OF ATTENTION OR PARTICIPATION.

RECOMMENDATION(S):

☑ MORE EFFORT   ☐ CONFERENCE WITH TEACHER   ☐ AFTER SCHOOL HELP: M TU W TH F   ☐ TUTORING

☐ *Present Grade F*

My "badge of honor" (redacted)

I later wrote of my attitude toward homework at the time: *Why am I doing this meaningless crap?* I shunned anything that disrupted my inner connection with God. It was not worth selling my soul for the world.[23] I pursued my spiritual discoveries at all costs, as nothing could compare to my inner explorations—an undertaking incalculably more meaningful than anything even remotely imaginable in life. My room likewise became a disorganized mess. I did not straighten it up; I just let it be, because I truly felt: So what? *Who cares?*—not me! I missed a couple of appointments as well. My new nocturnal prayer and meditation practices so diametrically opposed and took precedence over both my scholastic obligations and my worldly responsibilities that any secular ramifications simply did not concern me. I would let nothing sabotage my resolve or interrupt my focus. I sought lasting joy, not the mere fulfillment of fleeting obligations. As I wrote on December 12, 1974, "Life is a constant grab bag for temporary as opposed to eternal happiness." My undivided yearning for God caught hold of me on the deepest level and wouldn't let me go. I ruthlessly discarded all else.

After I meditated, I had no desire to engage in activity the next day. I felt I might lose whatever gems I had mined during my inner excursions the previous night. I wanted only to enjoy unruffled peace and bask in the blissful spiritual awareness that engulfed me. This pursuit had become my passion, drawing me deeper and deeper inward regardless of consequences. Nothing was more important. All that mattered was this newfound something growing inside me, which I nourished to the exclusion of everything else.

Upon waking the next morning, I would immediately catch my mind and stop it from functioning, forcing it to dwell in the present moment and remain immersed in the orb of inner silence that was increasingly growing inside me. This was difficult at first, because I met a wall of resistance from my stubborn mind, which did not want to be corralled in this manner. While my meditations were uniformly deep and fruitful, if I experienced anything that even remotely resembled a dry spell, this resistance was it. Each morning, my mind was bent on falling into its usual pre-spiritual-awakening habits and patterns, and it would have readily assumed the character traits and personality it had grown accustomed to adopting and embodying. But I forcibly intervened and broke these patterns through my repeated disruptions each morning, until I trained my mind to follow the new spiritual patterns I was determined to implement and enact. Body, mind, heart, and soul all became united one hundred percent, just as Jesus required,[24] in a grand symmetrical, orderly alignment, like a comet and its tail.

I ate no special diet, although I soon gave up meat. This had the effect of de-stimulating my body and mind, thus creating a calm psychophysical condition that was even more conducive to my spiritual practices. Along with becoming a vegetarian at the time, I felt that milk was the perfect food, as I hadn't yet developed lactose-intolerance at my young age. All told, I enjoyed a state of unusually keen mental clarity and robust physical wellbeing.

During the most intense phase of my awakening, I hardly ate at all, at times barely tasting food in my mouth until a strong inner sensation alerted me to stop. For some reason, this paltry amount of nourishment seemed to suffice, and I don't recall losing weight. Food became more and more irrelevant, almost an impediment. For that matter, I hardly slept. I somehow survived on pure spiritual energy that was derived from divine grace, and this would provide enough sustenance needed to maintain the intensity of my burgeoning realization.

I vividly remember one evening, October 31, when I drove my mother to the Daughters of Mary and Joseph Novitiate, which was then located on San Vicente Boulevard near the Santa Monica city limits. She had arranged to attend an event there that night. I then borrowed her car and picked up my friends Mark and Tim. It was Mark's birthday that day. I drove us all the way to Manhattan Beach, albeit along a kind of zigzag route because, well, I didn't have exact directions. My friends were getting hungry, and Tim was not amused by my circuitous wanderings: he was starving! Yet, I was neither affected by our delay nor stricken by hunger—my Awakening was cresting at the time. I clearly recall stopping at an intersection in Manhattan Beach, and a guy dressed as a vampire seated in a light blue VW bug turned and hissed at us (it was Halloween, and appropriately, the moon was full that night). We dined at a local eatery located on the Pacific Coast Highway, and my buddies gobbled their meals—a burger and a sandwich—but I refrained from eating meat. I also clearly recall foregoing turkey during our Thanksgiving meal that year, which surprised my mother. But I felt, as I later reflectively wrote, that I could "live on love." (I also did not want to have a Christmas tree that year, because I felt that chopping down trees was an "unjust exploitation of nature," as I wrote.)

Earlier that morning, before school began, I gave Mark a gift—my copy of the Moody Blues album *Every Good Boy Deserves Favour*. Offhand, this sounds like a backhanded gift, almost an insult—giving someone a used record. But there was a much greater significance to my gesture. This was the very same album I had listened to intensely from mid-September through October, and through my listening I attained a deep state of concentration. I felt the same intensity of my spirituality was imprinted on each groove of that album. Thus, this was actually the most meaningful gift I could have given him or anyone.

In a similar vein, I gave freely during this time without asking for anything in return. Possessions didn't matter—not even the Moodies' album, which had become, in many ways, a cherished part of my life. I felt that lines of demarcation and the very concept of ownership were inventions. I loaned my belongings to others, such as a Beatles' songbook I lent to Patrick, and I did not ask for them back. Sometimes when loaning my possessions to others, I didn't receive them back.

Artist's rendition of the *Sacred Heart of Jesus Statue* where I overturned my car at Sunset Boulevard and Marymount Place in the summer of 1974

As noted above, I borrowed my mother's car on Halloween and many other occasions during that time, because earlier that year, in around June, I rolled my beloved VW van when turning a corner too fast on famed Sunset Boulevard. I was then frustrated in my life—angry, restless, and no doubt searching for love and acceptance. Unlike those who never learn from such incidents, my accident did profoundly influence me: of all the places to come to a rest along the nearly 24-mile stretch of Sunset Boulevard, my van and I settled in the slow lane directly in front of and facing the outstretched arms of the statue of the Sacred Heart of Jesus, which, until it was relocated in 2020, stood as a beacon at the boundary of the Marymount High School campus. This experience was a precursor that pointed the way to what would soon unfold and would more than address my agitated mental state in the summer of 1974.

Throughout this time, with the exceptions noted below, I didn't seek outside help, look for gurus, or receive any type of spiritual initiations. Because of my youthful, provincial outlook and my correspondingly narrow experience of life, it never occurred to me to search out, for example, Hindu or Buddhist explanations, which may—or may not—have helped to place my experience in perspective. Except for adhering to the words of Jesus and the other passages I had read in the Bible, I embraced no formal belief system as my guidepost. I knew no theology; I could not define in intellectual terms what I was doing. I did not take philosophy or comparative religion classes or undergo prescribed religious practices. I could not explain the methods I used in light of the goals I sought to achieve; I doubt I could have articulated my objectives in any kind of formal theological context. My intention to dissolve my ego into the fathomless being of God thus remained unarticulated. It was more of a headlong thrust, a primal urge of the soul leaping into the void. I didn't read about this from any book; it sprang from my intense inner desire to be free and to disassociate my spiritual self from any sensation of isolation, of separateness. I was consumed with this burning wish to be free. Thus, I only followed my inner promptings, which I felt originated from God. I was fueled by raw feeling, entirely unrefined and unsophisticated, and invested with the full force of my being. I was totally on my own, learning the mysteries of my soul through my personal journey of self-discovery.

At most, I sought out two spiritual directors I had personally known, although I also briefly spoke with two priests. I felt that God and the state of spiritual oneness I experienced were not separate. I felt they were part of a single interrelated experience. I sought help from the experts I knew to explain my experience and to validate it.

First, I met with my Catholic grammar-school religion teacher at her home. I tried to articulate what I was undergoing. I spoke to her of experiencing a state with no pain, no worries, and uninterrupted peace. I tried to explain that not one event affected my true self, which I felt was composed of pure spirit.

She responded, "What you are describing to me is heaven."

I shared with her the following observation. "I feel if I were to be thrown out of a window off a high building, some part within me would not die, but would continue to live."

"Nonsense," she at once replied. "You would die instantly! If I were to pinch you, you'd feel that."

We continued our conversation along these lines, but she never accepted what I was undergoing, and thus, I felt she misinterpreted my experience. Because of the dramatic nature of my example, perhaps she thought she was talking me out of suicide.

But I truly identified with the shimmering, joyous essence that was taking hold inside my being. I also felt that my soul was located distinctly apart from my body, and so I didn't fear death, which I equated with the death of my body, not my spirit. I came to feel that it would be okay for anything to happen to my body, and regardless of whatever happened, my real "I"—my soul or spirit—would not die; my innermost spiritual "I" would be the same forever. Once during this time I signed my name, "I eternally exist," based on my experiential insight that my true "I" was neither my ego nor personality, nor body or matter, but pure disembodied spirit. I again wrote a note on December 4, "I think I would be able to live forever because I would have no use for this body."

My former religion teacher recommended that I read *Hymn of the Universe* by Jesuit philosopher Pierre Teilhard de Chardin, stating that my thoughts tallied with his. However, I did not read this book, not particularly on account of any perversity or rebelliousness, but because I could not tolerate blanketing an intellectual overlay on to my inner experience.

I also sought out an instructor at my high school, a priest, who taught religious studies, and, upon meeting with him, I related my experience. But as I described my spiritual state, I could see a certain look in his eyes that occurs when a person feels threatened. He responded by bringing up various theological points, which were well beyond my comprehension. He thereby intellectualized away my experience, which was the last thing I needed.

Neither of these religious counselors had any real idea what I was going through. They made no attempt to understand my experience, let alone authenticate it. And so I ran up against a brick wall. My experience was outside their frame of reference, their comfort zone, and the constraints imposed by their positions. They were both eager to explain away my situation, offering little if any genuine support and empathy that might have actually benefited me, or any insights that could have shed light on what I was experiencing.

Then again, what were they to do with a young, wild-eyed, would-be mystic who was breaking all boundaries of convention? However, their resistance or rejection of my experience didn't deter me one iota or shake the utter conviction I held that what I was experiencing was true, which I maintained until mid-December.

Other than sharing my experience with these two spiritual educators and briefly consulting the two other priests, I did not convey my inner findings to anyone. I once asked one of these priests, "Is there a God?" While he said, "Yes," he didn't give any pat answers but rather shared his personal experiences. I persisted: "How do you *know* there's a God?" He was stumped. He communicated his convictions and his doubts, but I sensed a more superficial, intellectually based faith that was not anchored in deeper experience. For me, experience was all that mattered. On approx. December 1, I tellingly wrote, "everything here is from personal experience and my impressions of these various experiences."

everything here is
from personal experience
and my impressions of
these various experiences.

Scan of original approx. December 1, 1974, holographic writing

I felt I knew the true message of Jesus, which I—a seventeen-year-old—could teach the Church. I never did so, but I truly felt I knew God better than these priests who vainly lectured about God without knowing God firsthand. I was prepared to straighten them out by proclaiming the truth about Jesus and setting them right. God was not to be found in some hastily written, disconnected Sunday sermon, because he was a living God of love and ever-new joy. I felt I could write books of love to people at all levels of understanding until they were in tune with the one Message Eternal. I felt such a strong connection with Jesus, as if I knew what he truly meant and these authority figures did not. They lectured and preached, whereas I practiced what Jesus taught. He was my closest friend. I lived a raw, wild spirituality, like John the Baptist.

I was also quite unaware of how my spiritual awakening might have affected others, except perhaps on one occasion. One day, I sat with a friend on the steps of a building at our high school during a break. Steve was an accomplished guitar player. He began playing his acoustic guitar, and I allowed my spiritual mood to overtake me. I also had brought my guitar to school that day, and I played rhythm to his lead. I became increasingly engrossed in his playing, as though I were deeply meditating on it. My spiritual mood apparently entwined both of us. Then, as if prompted by some mysterious inspiration, Steve began playing faster and faster. He perfectly, feverishly hit each arpeggiated note. When he concluded his frenzied solo, he looked at me with a broad smile and exclaimed in astonishment, "I've never played like that before!" This is the only instance I can recall when my spiritual mood may have spilled over and in some way affected another person.

While I wrote that I wanted at times to convey my spiritual experience to others by my touch, this never occurred as far as I could determine, and I was thus unable to transfer my inner state of consciousness onto others and thereby share it with them.

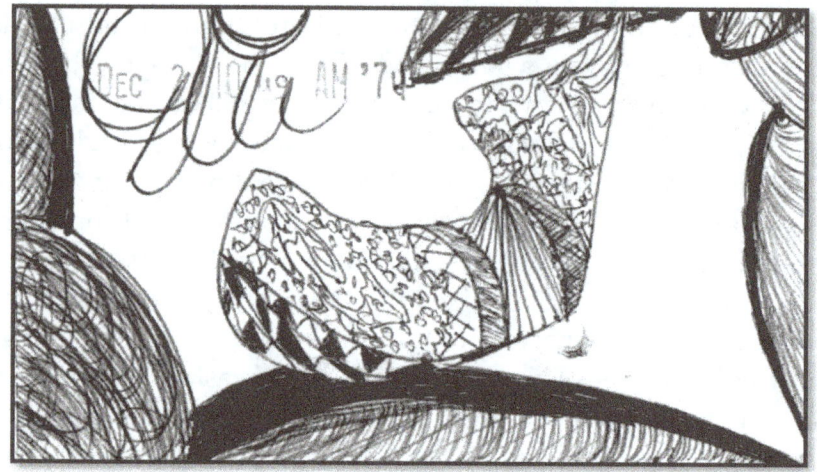

**I would often doodle in class and at home, at times drawing the
wild patterns that I was internally perceiving (see Appendix II).**

A Complete and Total Union Into One

Meanwhile, I continued my practices in solitude, feeling quite alone and isolated from others. At the same time, I felt the absolute truth of Jesus' counsel to "Love one another."[25] Along with putting into practice whatever biblical maxim I had read the previous night, the crux of my daily practice became invoking and expressing this increasing spiritual love, which I felt palpably coursing through my being. I extended this unconditional love to others, not so much through any particular act, but through my changed attitude. I became more open, sympathetic, friendly, nonjudgmental, and understanding. I tried to see the world from others' perspective. I deliberately broke down whatever barriers I sensed that might have prevented me from establishing a connection with other people at this deep, heartfelt level. I felt called, as if on a mission, to share this boundless spiritual love with all.

For example, as part of my inner discipline, I worked hard to rid myself of any hatred, bias, and animosity that I even remotely perceived within myself. The very ability to define an enemy or designate an adversarial situation became uprooted from the core of my being. I started to feel a deepening sympathy with all persons,

33

especially the destitute. I would vicariously experience the sorrows and afflictions of other people as if they were my own. I viewed strangers as my closest friends.

I never condemned others; the very ability to condemn was up-rooted within me, although I once corrected the ringleader of a small group of boys who got into the bad habit of spitting on other students. My reprimand was gentle, and he and his followers subsequently stopped their uncouth practice. I felt in many ways older, more adult than my peers, as though I had attained maturity. While I never embodied or touted any kind of self-righteous morality, I became incapable of doing harm, and I could see the ethical lapses of others as clearly as I could see my own. My guiding watchwords were "Do onto others"[26] and "Actions speak louder than words." Whenever I felt assailed by subtle tempta-tions, I would recall Jesus' injunction about choosing God or mammon.[27]

I didn't develop any kind of cosmology or eschatology; I was content with the practical advice given by Jesus on how to think and act in relation to the spiritual goals he advanced. On December 4, 1974, I enthusiastically wrote, "God is the union of the soul of a man before this ... body is selected to prove the soul of man in a material state!!!" This one-sentence summation was simple enough: during our time on earth, humans are meant to re-unite with God.

Because this universal love had such a vast equalizing effect on me, I felt I could mingle with rich and poor alike, treating them the same, unaffected by their social or economic status. I realized I was not superior to anyone, but rather equal with everyone. To think oth-erwise was the very pinnacle of arrogance—the presumption of the fallen angels. I came to realize that any condescending feelings I may have felt toward others were nothing more than a ruse of my ego. This stark insight had the effect of reducing my sense of self even more, as I continued to eliminate any arbitrary mental divisions that separated me from others. My thought processes came to be undefiled by the murkiness of self-interest and the discoloration of greed. My former calculating, self-seeking mind was fading into nonexistence. The graces that enveloped me enabled me to overcome these seemingly intractable, egotistical elements in my character.

My growing state of surrender also caused me to realize the van-ity of feeling sorry for others. One day I drove south with a friend,

Mark, on Veteran Avenue, preparing to turn east onto Ohio Avenue. Just before reaching the intersection, across the street in the northbound lane I spotted an ambulance with its lights flashing. The paramedics were assisting an old man who had been in some sort of accident. I began feeling waves of deep compassion toward him. Then, all of a sudden, in a flash, in a moment of utter clarity, I realized: Who am I to feel sorry for others? How dare I place myself in such a haughty position, deigning to bestow my gratuitous sympathy on "lesser" persons? All that I see—pain, suffering, death, starvation, joy: *everything*—is the way it should be. My genuine, moving concern and compassion for the poor and destitute helped to sustain the intensity of my spiritual practice; it gave me a cause that motivated me. But upon my epiphany, this underlying incentive simply vanished.

From that day forward during the time of my awakening, I no longer felt any sense of disparity in my attitude toward others. How proud I had been! I had always been trying to rearrange or alter events in order to vanquish that which I deemed "bad" or "evil." But this revelation burst my bubble. My so-called sympathy toward others was nothing but a selfish delusion. I realized in the very marrow of my being that all is *perfect as is*, without any further elaboration. This insight made me feel greatly humbled—a deep sense of humility—as I cast off all need to captain this world. I did not and could not control events. My attitude changed from one of attachment and aversion to things, to one of indifference and neutrality toward the things and events of this world. Such things simply didn't matter anymore.

And yet, I wasn't in any way cold or callous toward others, just the opposite. Consistent with my Aquarian nature, I radiated friendliness toward all, and I routinely greeted high-school friends with an affable "How ya doin'?" or, as appropriate, "Far out!" in keeping with the prevalent nomenclature of the day. I was warm and affectionate, often patting others on the shoulder or briefly touching their arm. I beamed a simple unlimited love toward all. My theology instructor remarked in class one day that I had "a beautiful smile" in front of the other students. My smile was genuine and spontaneous. I saw only the best and most sincere aspects of people, imputing on to them the very noblest of intentions. I was able to express spiritual love toward everyone without restriction, and give with a full, open heart. I knew no limitations, no distinctions. I was completely self-contained, filled with inconceivable joy, absorbed in inexpressible peace, and fundamentally receptive to and in tune with the words and teachings of Jesus, whose spirit became vibrantly alive in me.

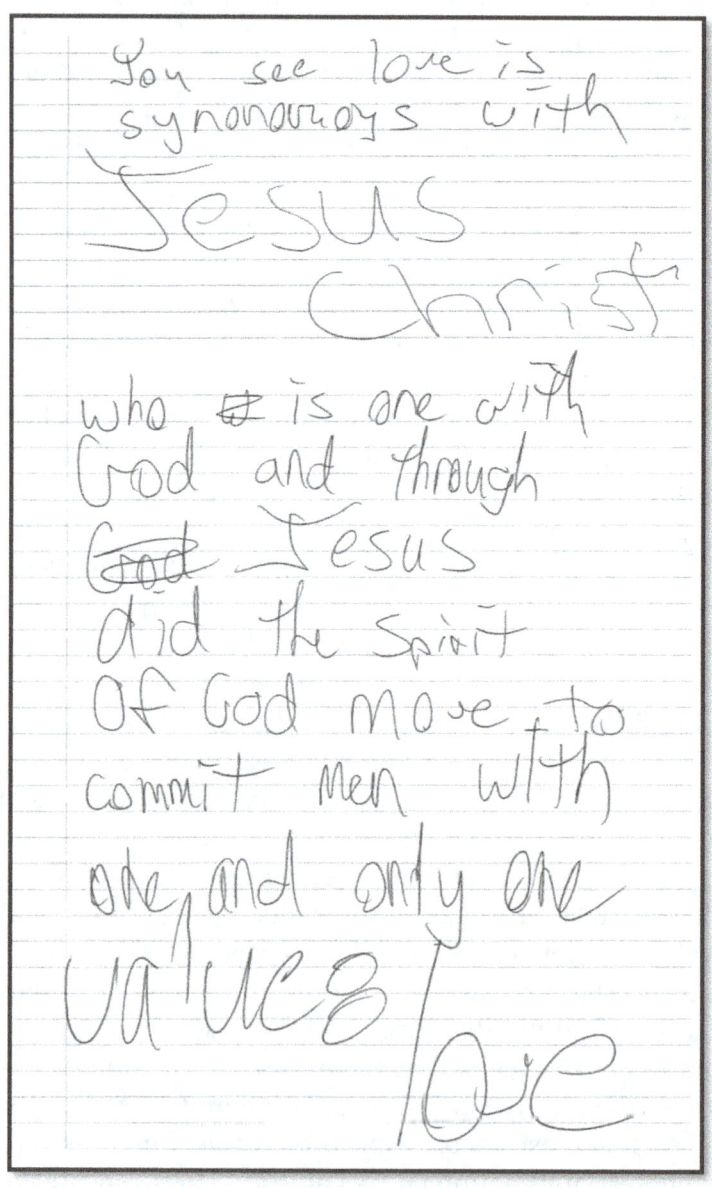

Scan of original December 4, 1974, holographic writing

I continued working on purging myself of nonproductive traits. Once I consciously recognized any attachments or addictions that may have been affecting me, I made deliberate efforts to break free from them, such as an occasional cigarette dependency I unfortunately acquired during my first year in high school, although I had sporadically smoked cigarettes beginning in my twelfth year. I had also tried cannabis, which was a popular psychoactive substance at that time with which many teens experimented. I remember one morning, sometime after the outset of my First Awakening, announcing to Matt, one of the boys who carpooled with me to high school, that I had given up smoking pot. There is one paramount reason why I had quit at that time: the spiritual experience I underwent was far more refined, far more subtle than any state that could be induced by marijuana. In fact, pot only served to obscure and diminish the clarity and immediacy of my luminous spiritual experience. Pot was coarse and murky by comparison; it muddled and muddied my direct perception of the spiritual reality. I could achieve on my own the altered state that cannabis approximated, only the state that I attained without marijuana was far superior because it was exponentially purer. Thus, I had no need for it; I had outgrown it. As my spiritual experience grew, my whole being became more and more refined. My mind became more subtle in all aspects, as it climbed an upward ascent beyond the intellect to an abode of pure, imageless joy.

And so I forcibly attempted to give up familiar habits, accustomed routines, and deep-seated patterns of behavior. For instance, my friends fully expected me to stay up late and watch David Bowie, one of my principal early 1970s musical heroes, when he appeared on *The Dick Cavett Show* on December 5, 1974. But, obeying my inner spiritual promptings, I went to bed earlier than usual that night after my meditation routine, and I missed the program, much to their subsequent chagrin. Yet, I didn't feel that I missed out on something. I was attuned to the Lord's will, which caused me far greater joy. My spiritual focus consumed my entire being, and this provided the impetus for me to attach or detach myself at will completely from all things, such as watching TV shows and viewing artists I admired.

No doubt my peers must have been mystified by my abrupt, uncharacteristic behavioral changes. Along with giving up meat, I began cutting my own hair. A couple of acquaintances criticized my actions. I don't doubt they looked on me as enigmatic, unorthodox, and nonconformist—which I unpretentiously took as compliments. One friend, Kelly, once told me that I gave off "bad vibes," presumably because I rarely spoke with him compared to our previous loquacious interactions; he was undoubtedly puzzled. But this didn't phase me. A classmate criticized me for "always wearing the same clothes" to class, which I answered with silence and a smile.[28] This was very much in keeping with what I wrote on September 13, 1974, where I aspired to let "other people's actions ... not bother me."

I also wrote on September 13 that I would "not conform to other people's thinking—doing what they want me to." This antiauthoritarian principle guided and dictated my behavior. I wrote on one submitted classroom assignment, concerning "following orders: if I [were] to join the Navy, I'd be 'brigged' within about twelve hours!!!" I was even more rebellious on November 12, when I wrote, "I refuse to do this assignment ..." However, my defiant attitude had manifested as early as March 1974, when, as a junior, I submitted an unsolicited critique of my classroom assignment in which I minced no words: "I refuse to do this pure unadulterated BULLSH*T ... This is ridiculous." Fortunately, the easygoing instructor didn't report me to the dean.

At the very beginning of my awakening, likely around the first week of September, I remember accompanying a friend to see the movie *Death Wish*. But I literally walked out during the gruesome opening scenes; I simply could no longer tolerate subjecting my mind to such depictions of brutality and violence. I'm sure my actions upset my friend, who wanted to view this film. I had also grown more sensitive following my eleven-day High Sierra trip, and this change significantly affected how much I would thereafter allow worldly things to impinge on my mind.

These are examples of the general unsympathetic reception I received during my spiritual awakening, owing to others' complete lack of understanding of what I was undergoing, coupled with their unwillingness even to attempt to grasp it. Beyond that, I was reticent to speak to anyone about what I was experiencing. And so, while I maintained contact with a handful of close friends—Mark, Tim, Doug, and Jeffrey—some friends fell by the wayside. But I genuinely didn't care what those former friends or my critics or any of my other acquaintances thought. If they thought me crazy, I thought them even crazier. I felt my behavior was consistent, as I no longer followed the predictable patterns of people. I was now following a higher authority.

Likewise with my family. My parents had divorced in the early Seventies after my graduation from grammar school, and I lived at home with my mother and older sister during my high-school years. Now, my mother was always a good person—scrupulous, caring, thoughtful, and deeply concerned about our welfare. But during my First Awakening, I saw her as the very personification of the Devil. (For that matter, I viewed most anything that pulled me away from my inner state as originating from the Devil.) I felt that she was clinging and continually nagging me, seemingly with the willful intent of intruding into my life and doing everything in her power to drag me from my spiritual state. While Jesus was chronicled to have counseled, "Whoever comes to me and does not hate their father and mother and wife and children and brothers and sisters, and further, even their own life—they cannot be my disciple,"[29] he also emphasized that we must "Love one another."[30] But this was difficult to practice when it came to my mother. When I felt her nagging became excessive, I'd sometimes bellow, "Stop bugging me!" during my early- and mid-teens. However, when I grew older, I could clearly see that she was a giving, generous soul, and she unswervingly supported and encouraged my various projects in life, including my later spiritual investigations. But she tended to smother me with an overbearing kind of love, which I resented when seeking my independence.[31] Still, she was a pivotal figure, and I benefitted throughout my life from her selfless example.

At some point, I reached a state wherein I experienced no anxieties and no worries. I embraced each event as it played out, without fretting, feeling that God was directing everything that was occurring. This realization humbled me. I felt, *Who am I to interfere with the ways of God?* As a result, I began to see perfection in all things without any need to intervene and change them. My change in attitude corresponded timewise with my visceral realization on Veteran Avenue described above. I welcomed all I encountered with nonjudgmental acceptance; I saw all circumstances entirely as they were, without embellishments.

I realized there was very little I could do to alter most events anyway, so I decided: Why should I worry about them? It seemed fruitless to stew over this situation or that outcome. It was only my body—the seat of my ego—that was going through the various activities of life.

Because God was in charge, I felt I should accept as God's will whatever developed unsought, on its own, without trying to bring about a different result that would be more advantageous to my ego. I saw that everything was perfect as it is without any need to alter it whatsoever; each event unfolded the way it was supposed to, so I simply fit in and flowed with events. Whatever presented itself, I accepted. Whatever I lacked was neither missed nor desired. This attitude imbued me with utter peace of mind. My watchwords from that point on became, as I had written at the time, "nothing matters," because I stopped assigning a hierarchy of importance—viewing some things as more favorable, and other things as less favorable—to the various circumstances of my life.

An uncanny intuitive sense overtook me whereby I seemed to know what to say and do in all situations. Other than attending prearranged activities, I never plotted my courses of action ahead of time; whatever I did was entirely unplanned. Every choice I made appeared to be the perfect course of action to take—no more, no less. I didn't spend my energy thinking out things; my decisions were in-the-moment, spontaneous. I felt fully satisfied with any given experience; I had no unfulfilled desires, no lingering sense of frustrated goals. In this manner, as a serendipitous side-effect, unbounded energy was released by virtue of my not trying, not thinking, and not planning.

Thus, I neither strove to attain a particular goal nor did I bemoan whatever was absent from my life, including things I did not possess. I felt I didn't own anything; yet everything was mine. I felt there was nothing more in life to be sought or achieved. I felt my purpose in life was fulfilled at all times. Events either would or wouldn't come to pass, and so I purposely avoided dwelling on them. In addition, I disciplined myself not to complain about anything, which imbued me with endless patience. It was infinitely more valuable for me to retain my inner calm than to disturb it for worldly purposes, such as complaining about this or that. For example, my mother packed my daily lunch for me, which invariably consisted of a scant slab of peanut butter coupled with a dribble of jam on Oro-weat whole-wheat bread—a rather ghastly affair. But I never complained about this somewhat unpalatable gastronomical nutriment or other things or events, if I even noticed any seeming insufficiencies in them. The very concept of "sufficiency" was becoming increasingly difficult for me to judge and determine.

Because of my resolve, I would not tolerate even a ripple of distress entering my being. Nothing worried or alarmed me, although at first, I wasn't so unflappable. If, for instance, a telephone rang right next to me, it may have startled me, but later I was unshakable. I did not resist anything, even if I was criticized or slighted. I simply didn't react. I felt all to be God's will, and I found my repose within. I was wrapped in the unswayable contentment of inwardly generated peace. And so, I simply would not allow any such distractions to pull me away from my spiritual practices. One moment's diversion brought me the pain of a thousand hells. I viewed every circumstance as a trial in which I was challenged either to remain in harmony with God or else forfeit my inner relationship with him.

I also became receptive to anything that would help me grow spiritually. I considered everything—past incidents, encounters with people, current events—as *lessons* designed to bring me closer to God. I could either resist learning from them or cooperate with them. But because I viewed all things as my teacher, I accepted them as challenges for me to go beyond myself. With my changed attitude, I was able to look on all former difficulties and unpleasant situations as tests of my patience, forbearance, and faith. I tried to imbibe a given lesson once, so that its principle sank deep and became part of my psyche. Thus, I welcomed these lessons, likening them to spiritual tests, and I humbled myself in order to learn them. Occasionally, I actually sought humiliating experiences in order to subdue my ego and learn humility. Many times an appropriate lesson or teaching appeared out of nowhere. I viewed my past in a new light by seeing how all the elapsed situations in my life, both good and bad, were really learning experiences intended to help me find God.

Similarly, I found meaning in anything that crossed my path—listening to songs, encountering people, driving in traffic. By viewing all events and people as teachers, I was able to see benefits in every situation, even so-called "bad" circumstances. I thereby learned to find God in ordinary things. For example, I would analogize ordinary love songs into a yearning not for the love interest in the song, but for God. My heart was an open book, and I divested myself of all preconceived notions and embodied the attitude of one as if learning for the first time.

Neurologists have discovered that, as humans grow older, they process information in a manner that builds on prior experiences by recognizing and organizing them. The brain works to patternize such experiences, which means in practical terms that we become jaded insofar as we forget what it's like to undergo the wonder and curiosity we once felt when growing up. But my neurons were impeded, as it were, and this process of patternization simply ceased to function. I never felt jaded, as in "I've seen this all before." On the contrary, everything I experienced was as if for the first time. Life was brand new to me. All things I encountered thus brought me face to face with the inescapable God I so earnestly sought. I detected the underlying oneness in each and every event and thing I came across.

During this period, I found very few outside interests with which I could relate. This was because my new spiritual world became increasingly disconnected from the secular world I once knew and inhabited. One day at home, I viewed a TV showing of the 1933 film version of *Alice in Wonderland*. I felt a deep connection with Alice's illogical adventures and the assortment of eccentric characters she encountered. Everything in her Rabbit Hole world was as topsy-turvy and nonsensical as what I was facing in mine. I fully empathized with Alice's identity crisis: "I can't explain *myself*, I'm afraid, sir," said Alice, "because I'm not myself, you see."[32]

And, like the Private Charles Plumpick character in the 1966 cult-classic *King of Hearts*, I discovered that those who were considered insane were often saner than those who declared them so and who themselves were considered "sane." Again, I could relate to Patrick McGoohan's ever-defiant "Number Six" character from the 1967–68 TV series *The Prisoner*, and also free-spirited Lucas Jackson from 1967's *Cool Hand Luke*, both of whom proved that those who refuse to conform are often the most rational of all.

This same reasoning applied to David Bowie's powerful 1970 song "All the Madmen," whose protagonist is characterized as preferring the company of those deemed mad to the company of so-called normal men because he is convinced the madmen all share his same degree of sanity. I, too, was mad—mad for God—and I would not compromise my spiritual madness simply to appease the truly insane, who wandered free in the world and controlled the fate of the rest of us. Because the axis of my inner being was now centered so radically apart from mainstream society, I had envisioned the possibility of being dragged off to an insane asylum, as I would not compromise myself for the world, or seek its approval, or explain or justify my inner state. I was my own person—whole, intact, self-contained.

As my awakening continued to unfold, each day I awoke to a new level of understanding. Upon rising, I mustered up all my energy and forced my wandering mind back into focus, so I could return to the state of inner silence I had attained the previous night. I literally forced myself to focus on even the most mundane activities, such as when dialing telephone numbers. My mind was concentrated to the utmost degree. Because of the intensity of my practice, I attained a steady mind that no longer wandered. I not only mercilessly thrust out all thoughts but I summoned into my heart a tangible experience of the living Jesus. In this manner, I curbed all mental processes and firmly directed my attention back to my spiritual goal, which was, as I had written on approx. December 1, "a complete and total union into One … a totally perfected state of Divine Love and knowledge of nothing else."

Using my willpower, I visualized Jesus as my constant companion, alongside me whenever walking, seated next to me when driving, and present with me when doing anything.[33] This sustained visualization of Jesus accompanying me everywhere vastly strengthened my faith and increase my fearlessness, for it had the effect of smothering any doubts that might have crept in to undermine my spiritual experience. As my whole universe then centered around Jesus, my faith grew to the extent that I *knew* he existed. I strongly felt his invisible presence, and I would mentally converse with him in ongoing inner communications.[34] In this manner, I cultivated and developed a deep, abiding, intimate relationship with Jesus. Because of this deep relationship, it felt as though I were carried on a wave of pure incandescent love. Unending portals of joy opened up inside me.

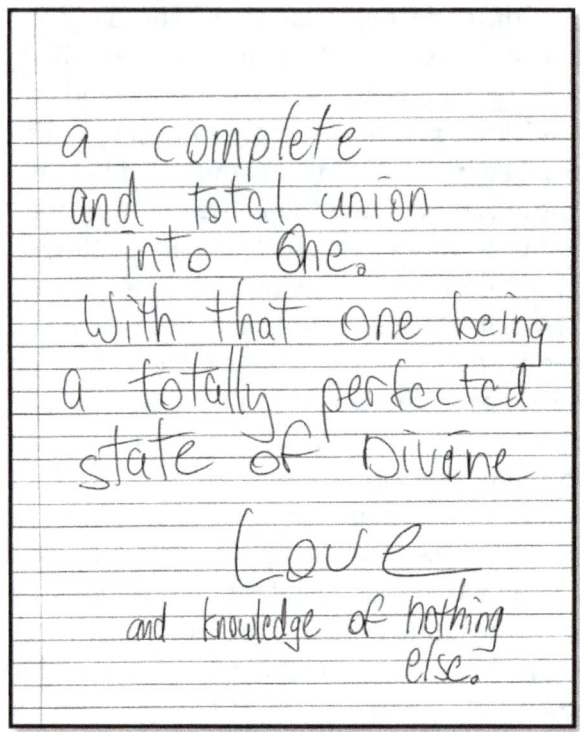

a complete
and total union
into one.
With that one being
a totally perfected
state of Divine

Love

and knowledge of nothing
else.

Scan of original approx. December 1, 1974, holographic writing

September soon turned into October, and I became even more intensely seized by a burning desire to be free. This passionate yearning gnawed at me to the exclusion of all else. It continually uplifted me. This had the effect of strengthening my intentions all the more. I maintained my fervent aspirations day and night, clinging to it tenaciously at all costs. I attempted to adhere round-the-clock to my spiritual ideals without once compromising them. My resolute intentions helped me to stay on track so I wouldn't be diverted. I would allow nothing to sabotage my resolve. I kept moving onward and upward, spiraling higher and higher, never settling for mediocrity or resting in smug self-assuredness. I honed myself on the whetstone of my undeviating spiritual goal, and I continuously strained and pressed forward to achieve it.

During this progressively wondrous time, I made every effort to be guided solely by God. Whatever decisions I made seemed just right insofar as I didn't feel that I made them; I felt they originated from God, and I perfectly surrendered to them and thus I never lost my inner peace when following them. Moreover, a distinct inner voice emerged, which I sensed more as interior proddings than audible vocalizations, and I forced myself to obey it. The overarching theme it conveyed to me was to reject the world and undistractedly focus on God. In so many words, this message repeated itself throughout different situations every day. The guidance given by my inner voice frequently resulted in depriving me of what I might otherwise would have wanted to occur, or else it contradicted what I might have expected to take place. This created in me a keen sense of detachment by deflating my sense of ego and bringing what I once avoided on equal terms with what I once cherished. Thus liberated from my personal desires, I experienced a perpetual state of contentment. I felt inwardly fulfilled, ever at peace. I was never steered into any harmful circumstances when following the protective goadings of my mystical inner voice. Situations were often intuitively, mysteriously explained to me by it.

When interacting with people, I saw, related to, and communicated with their spiritual essence, connecting with the deepest part of their soul. I projected the spiritual awareness I experienced on to them and spoke to them with complete familiarity, as though they were my dearest, most intimate friend. I was not nervous, apprehensive, or anxious with others because I felt that we shared the same consciousness; that we were inwardly one. When others spoke, I often felt it was I who was talking. The ability to perceive others as objects distinct from my own soul had vanished: we shared a singular infinitude of consciousness. I accepted all they said without judgment, all the experiences they related as if my own, all their concerns as if deeply meaningful to me. I tuned in to the undercurrent of any given person, thus instantly establishing a rapport with them, which made them feel totally at ease. I identified so closely with their thoughts that many times I felt as if there were an intermingling of minds wherein any distinction between their mind and my mind did not exist. The thoughts of others took root in my mind as if they were my very own; I would often finish their sentences and sometimes even vocalize their unspoken thoughts.

Once, when driving with Tim, I fully allowed this merger to occur. It was as if one person were speaking; some of our exchanges took place in unison. I assumed ownership of his thoughts, as if his were mine and mine his, whereby any distinct localization was lost. My mind had ascended to a more subtle realm than ever before. This was not caused by any kind of pathological psychological state, but rather a heightened supernatural nondual spiritual experience.

I also felt that others were clued in on some grand cosmic secret, only they were merely acting out a role, pretending to be this or that person. In my mind, I thought they knew that this world and all the situations in life were a big farcical game of sorts. I could never be sure. Their guises and secular identities were just one big masquerade. It was as if they were already in sync with the spiritual core of creation—as if they were already fully enlightened—and it was only I who was catching on late. I had, in fact, mentally extended the spiritual consciousness I experienced within myself onto other people, and thus I could clearly see God in them, just as I had found God inside myself.

When people conversed with me, I felt as though they were talking to someone else, referring to someone else, someone besides me, from whom I was different, because my personality had become so attenuated that I ceased to identify with my ego or body.[35] When responding to others, I spoke and acted extemporaneously without first thinking or gathering my thoughts or mentally rehearing my words beforehand. I didn't always directly address questions posed to me by others, which must have baffled them. But I often saw beyond their questions and tuned in to their undertone, their underlying need or hidden motive, which is what I would actually address.

One time, a high-school friend, Jake, innocently wondered why I used "such big words." But words, however big or small, spontaneously flowed out of my mouth when warranted, and sentences arranged themselves and ideas articulated themselves as if out of thin air throughout the time of my awakening. They were clearly formed ideas, always exact and appropriate to the situation, as were the volume of words. Further, my economy of words was direct and to the point; I never beat around the bush or cushioned my words with needless verbiage or descriptors. I made logical presentations from beginning to end. I could see the overview and essence of each argument. I reasoned from the subtlest points. I could trace all things to one or two main principles. Still, I vastly preferred silence to speech, and I rarely spoke unless absolutely necessary. I truly felt there was no need for speaking, which seemed burdensome. I became especially silent and inwardly centered.

Even though I went through the motions of attending my daily high-school classes, I rarely socialized during this time, and I was not dating, neither was I in any sexual relationship, although I had to cope at times with the overwhelming concupiscence that can and does often befall hormone-drenched teenage boys. Still, I viewed these sensations as fundamentally not different from my nondual spiritual experiences insofar as both served as vehicles to throw off every last vestige of separation and blot out all self-consciousness until a complete loss of self was attained.

I tried not to taint my mind with worldliness, which is why I largely kept to myself. I shared my experiences with God when praying in secret, and I shunned anything that would draw attention to my spiritual practices. I did not strive for recognition, which I found repugnant. Just the opposite—I attempted to remain anonymous. I didn't disturb others, but rather let them alone. Likewise, I didn't want to be disturbed. I didn't try to impress others. I acted anonymously and felt repugnance at the thought of seeking credit or honor. I followed Jesus' teaching vis-à-vis, "Your Father, who sees in secret ..."[36]

During lunch at school or if I had spare time between classes, I would routinely wander off and hang out by myself on a secluded lawn area, amid scenic plantings of trees and a colorful bed of roses, on the far side of the school grounds near the rectory—the least populated section of campus—rather than mingle with classmates. I couldn't wait to remove my shoes so that I could sit barefoot on the grass and simply *be* in boundless joy. I totally identified with nature, so I felt right at home.

Realizing there were essentially none who understood or supported my spiritual efforts, I was content with exploring my inner world alone and, for the most part, sequestering myself from other people wherever possible. My room at home served the same purpose. It had become my personal place of worship where I could unfold the secrets of my soul in solitude. As I wrote on September 14, 1974, "I want to be alone, enclose myself in four walls." My spirit required this seclusion. It journeyed on endless reverberations of ecstatic silence. God was reshaping my very being.

All I wished for was Love. Period.
Scan of original approx. December 1, 1974, holographic writing.

I Am All I See

November to early December 1974 marked the most intense phase of my First Awakening. I constantly felt alive in the bliss-filled state that enfolded me. Because of my ongoing practice of meditation, I soon left behind the realm of thoughts and concepts entirely. An inner stillness swept over me, which enabled me to perceive each instant, seemingly every nanosecond, apart from all mental filters, conjectures, and interpretations. I was fully present at all times—immersed in a seizing in-the-moment intensity that results when the mind is freed of all thoughts. There was no continuity of experience from one moment to the next—all such partitions dissolved. I experienced no limitations, no boundaries.

On approx. December 1, I wrote, "Everything is relative. Beauty is in the eye of the beholder. ... Heaven and hell are relative. Good and bad are different things to different people. ... Finite and infinite are all relative to the definer." I had the revelation that all words and definitions were arbitrary and relative to those who use them. Yet, the underlying absolute Reality itself remains unaltered.

Time as we know it did not exist. It was broken down into the minutest of particles, each a whole universe unto itself and unrelated to the particle just past or the one yet to come. I had no sense of past or future; there was no linkage between moments—only the present moment existed, and this same moment extended into infinity. This eternal now was all that occurred; it was all-consuming. All else was imaginary. The past became irrelevant; the future didn't have any substance. Life was created anew each pulsating second. No two experiences, however similar, were exactly alike, as Heraclitus sagely observed when he wrote, "You cannot step into the same river twice" (from *Cratylus* by Plato), which tallied exactly with my experience. For example, I felt that, though warm food got cold, cereal became soggy, and so forth, and thus things changed, there was an underlying Essence that did not decay. I felt this underlying essence within me, and I extended this inner awareness and projected it onto outer things.

I didn't start or finish any activity as we commonly understand these terms; I merely joined in at a certain point. As I was fully present in any given moment, nothing really began or ended. I simply experienced an ever-changing display of unrelated events tied together by a foundational unity. Once when running the kitchen faucet, I perceived the flowing water as if gazing into its molecular structure, as if it were liquid infinity streaming out of the faucet, while at the same time I saw the water wholly captured in the moment, as if only that moment existed. I was thoroughly immersed in a non-intellectual intensity of focused attention that locked me into the present tense. This produced a continuum of heightened joy. My perceptions of the past also became seemingly unbounded, stretched by elasticity, as time ceased to exist and all time-constricted dividers between events dissolved. I was inextricably linked to each instant as a totality in itself with nowhere else to go. I never lost my bearings or became disoriented. My mind became unfrozen, uncompartmentalized; I experienced no dichotomy or division of time, which had lost its imprisoning grip.

Yet, paradoxically, I came to feel there was all the time in the world. I grew younger, became simpler. The world had become too large for me. By shutting myself up in my room, I was able to explore a smaller, more manageable world—my own inner world, with which I was becoming increasingly familiar. My true self, my soul, was being revealed, and this new spiritual dimension produced an aura of enchantment within me woven with dimensions of meaning. I thrived on simplicity, and I pared all complications away to nothingness. My life had become God-driven, not clock-driven.

During my awakening, I became imbued with feelings of the innocence, wonder, and wellbeing inherent in my early childhood. My memory became exceptionally clear, and I experienced a myriad of flashbacks from my childhood; I relived numerous emotions and the actual moods that accompanied events from my past as they replayed themselves in my mind's eye, mostly joyous. This tremendous sense of carefree contentment, security, and safety became integrated into my then-present consciousness. I became childlike in many ways. This helped to usher out all negative emotions, which vanished over time as I shed their shadowy influence. As I divested myself of layer upon layer of my old, encrusted self, I would repent at a visceral level for having ever forsaken my soul, at times crying out in humility to God, "I was wrong!" In many ways, I cried away my past.

At the same time, I felt an invisible Presence—God—was present during all the events of my past, even the most embarrassing, where God looked on ever silently. God's loving Presence would infuse my mind whenever cavalcades of past images paraded across the screen of my consciousness. In this way, my past became transformed. I vividly saw that God was unequivocally present throughout all my past circumstances, accepting and forgiving me, thereby allowing me to accept and forgive myself. I was enveloped in awe and simply gave thanks.

Equally paradoxically, I felt older, ancient, timeless. I felt at home everywhere. Nothing seemed distant or apart from me; I experienced no sense of separation between the things I observed and my inner self. I later wrote of my experience at the time, "I am one. I am ageless. I am all I see." I also wrote on December 12, 1974, "It is as if I am one with all."

Everything I came across appeared vibrant and intensely alive. I often sensed a wondrous orb of misty, haloed light that shone around objects. When traveling about, I would see trees, rose bushes, and other living things vibrating with refulgent life, radiating the infinite light of God. Objective reality was aglow with a living, vital force, as I told one of the priests at my high school. My vision corresponded to the insightful verse by Elizabeth Barrett Browning:

Earth's crammed with heaven,
And every common bush afire with God.[37]

At times, I felt as if I were perceiving the innermost structure of things, composed of scintillating energy, and not their outer form. I would see the world around me as shimmering waves of bliss, similar to when watching tall meadow grasses swaying rhythmically in the wind, or when viewing a grove of weeping birches quaking gently in the breeze—each tree melding into a grand ensemble of translucent swells dancing in unison. In fact, all my sense perceptions were heightened. I would hear the tiniest nuances of sounds. The fresh sensation of *listening* to the sonic soundstage of life, devoid of any mental interpretations, brought the finest, most subtle details to such sounds as the wind rustling through trees or birds chirping on my back porch. I could hear what seemed like the first time in my life the delicate sounds of sprinklers in motion, which created layer upon layer of discreet acoustics. I was thus able to discern an acute division of aural sensations, and I could source the location of the minutest distinction of sound.

The same occurred with any visual landscape before me. I vividly recall seeing the second October nearly full moon while standing on the porch in my backyard. As I stared in wonder, I lost all sense of separation between the moon and my sense of self—"moon is my mind," as I later wrote—the two had merged, as my "I" had vacated my being and no intervening element existed within. Likewise, I merged and became one, as it were, with the essence of stars, oleander bushes, or whatever occupied my vision.

My other senses became equally sharp. I could *smell* the smog in the foul L.A. air. My tactile sense grew extraordinarily sensitive. Sometimes I could taste textures and feel sounds, a form of synesthesia that strangely manifested on occasion. What I was seeing, or hearing, or feeling, nobody else saw or heard or felt. Yet, I knew what I was experiencing was real, perhaps the most real.

These experiences were not caused by ingesting or inhaling any kind of psychotropic substance or by any other physical means; they stemmed from an exponentially purer and far more powerful source: they originated as graces from God, combined with a fully concentrated mind. I would witness similar serendipitous mystical occurrences, which I similarly attributed to God. I saw the world with new eyes. I felt I had encountered perfection.

I was deeply inspired and motivated by Jesus' directive not to judge or to measure, which made a profound impact: "Judge not that you not be judged. For in the same manner you judge, you will be judged. And with whatever measure you use, it will be used to measure you."[38] I looked up the words "judge" and "measure" in the dictionary and analyzed their deeper meanings. I concluded that Jesus intended for us to root out the very mechanism within us that is responsible for judgment and measurement, definition and categorization. Thereafter, I made a determined effort to completely stop these mental functions.

Accordingly, I would command my body and mind to remain entirely calm and relaxed when meditating. I would catch any thoughts immediately upon detection, then visualize them being hurled away from me. In essence, I figuratively prevented them from entering my skull. I concomitantly banished all emotions, especially toxic emotions, such as fear, worry, doubt, regret, and concern about what others might think of me. I thereby arrested all inner chatter by using the sheer force of my will to control my mind. This had the effect of subduing the talkative voice inside my brain and evicting any and all thoughts *before* they had a chance to fully materialize and catch hold. As a result, I largely lost the ability to classify, differentiate, and compartmentalize things, as the unseen boundary that separated my ego from the objects I perceived began to disappear. I cast aside all labels, all definitions. The mental faculty responsible for judgment and measurement thus became suspended during my meditations, and soon this carried over into my waking activities. All became the same for me. Everything was equal in value and equal in importance. The ability to compare no longer existed in me. My rational mind ceased to function as before; nothing made "sense" anymore. The continuity of normal mental processing had stopped, and what formerly connected "this" with "that" now produced a vacuum of endless empty space: nothing registered anymore.

What in fact I was doing was dismantling the functional parts of my mind. I picked apart these components—intellect, memory, emotions, the faculty of judgment—and shut them down until I suppressed their ability to function autonomously. I also didn't do anything to address any emotional problems that emerged. Instead, I *unmasked* any subconscious fears and other emotions that had dictated my reactions. I no longer perfunctorily reacted to external stimuli: I paused, so to speak; I was in control. I became unflappable, settled in the infinity of the moment, never swayed from my central bearing, which was fixed in God, where I had unshakably anchored my inner being. I felt settled, entirely at home in that state.

After I was able to detect then peel back and expose a particular emotion, it ceased to influence me. It simply lost its power as the intensity of my spiritual experience overshadowed its grip and even its relevance. I thereby muzzled many unconscious reactions that heretofore ran on autopilot, and I suspended the operations of any number of deep-rooted behavior patterns. As a result of disassociating myself from the influence of these inner emotions, I came to neither regret nor doubt anything, as regret and doubt no longer existed in my mindstream. All anxiety and stress reactions were gone. I felt no want, fear, or need.

Likewise, I exposed many hidden assumptions. I also uncovered then halted the workings of any fixed habits that were lurking in my mind. I soon was able to disengage from the usual ways in which I interacted with others. For example, when conversing with others, I didn't always look them directly in the eye. In one of the shortcomings to my progress that I never addressed, I felt self-conscious when looking at other people, concerned that they might see the wild spiritual intensity that had gripped me. I could entirely relate to David Bowie's poignant and, as especially applied to me, prophetic lyrics about eyes from his 1969 song "Wild Eyed Boy From Freecloud."

In a similar vein, once I visited my friend Jeffrey and listened intensely to what he was saying, but all the while I was absorbed in watching the endlessly captivating formations of bubbles in his aquarium. While seated in one classroom, I would piercingly stare out the open door, not always due to boredom, but mainly because I was totally absorbed in my interior spiritual state, and the view outside of nature comported more with my inner vision than a chalkboard. Fortunately, the laidback, somewhat avant-garde instructor didn't call me out for what might be perceived as my daydreaming during class.

Moreover, I thought in different patterns. I forced myself to experience things that were heretofore unfamiliar, such as using my left hand to perform routine functions for which I would normally, and unconsciously, use my right hand. I correspondingly made myself sit or lie down in different positions, with which I was unaccustomed, because they were entirely new. I was no longer running on autopilot. I made sure that everything I did was always fresh, never familiar or rote. I broke all patterns, ruthlessly tearing down the encrusted inner edifices and conditioning from my past. I swept aside whatever dusty inner debris I could find that reeked of habituation. I had thus effectively deconstructed and reverse-engineered my own mind so it would no longer automatically function and control me. I did all this in service of my soul, which I was liberating by wrenching it free from the clutches of my mind.

During my prayerful supplications, I tangibly invoked the heavenly Father, visualizing His loving presence spreading through my being, then around my body, encompassing my room, my house, my neighborhood, and beyond. Simultaneously, I mentally created a protective "force field" composed of God, which I envisioned as a circular sphere-like ball that radiated an aura around me, my room, and my house, sheltering us in a projected shield of safety, which cast out all fear and blotted out all thoughts, worries, and concerns. Only God was allowed inside this protective sphere. I felt completely safe within this spiritual force field; my "I" was neither affected by nor involved in any adverse or confrontational situations.

My nighttime meditations deepened. Increasingly, it would take very little time for me to enter my state of inner quietude, which I craved more than anything. Eventually, I acquired the perspicacity, the mental stamina, the focus, the resolve, and was granted the grace to dismiss thoughts at will, without all the effort formerly required. I monitored my mind, and if any thought arose, I immediately traced it back to its source and quashed it.[39] Then I would bring this inner monitoring process to a standstill by stopping it so that no activity remained in my mind. Once all the mentations and images ceased, I was bathed in a sublime silence. I had found a place inside myself untouched by any agitation, and I allowed nothing to breach this inner sanctum. I aggressively threw off all psychological hindrances and forced myself to abide in a state without thoughts while I simultaneously poured out an aching heart of innocent, untarnished love into the very soul of God.

At the height of my awakening, I felt completely elevated, transported to an otherworldly domain. I became steeped in a transcendent luminosity, consumed by the effulgent presence of God. This was an altogether different realm. My mind was stilled, my emotions quieted. Through my intense effort coupled with God's grace, my spirit was cracking through and disintegrating the shell of my ego—my former self—and emerging into a totally new life. I experienced unending, indescribable peace. The barrier between matter and spirit had ruptured, enabling me to peer at life from the other side of reality. Whatever tenuous grip the outer world still held on me started to loosen. I could no longer recognize my former self, which was receding out of existence. I was riding on the continuum of eternity. I lived in an abode of undiluted happiness. I was being transformed by God. I felt that if others were to experience these same feelings of unmitigated joy, they couldn't withstand the accompanying euphoria, and they would cry aloud in ecstasy when so utterly relaxed and saturated with the blissful torrents pouring through their organism.

These feelings humbled me, and I would exclaim with emotion, "Thank you, Lord" when the uprushing sensations of unutterable peace and ecstasy, combined with a total lack of anxiety, coursed and surged through my being. I felt as though all my worldly travails had ended. I felt totally free. I had no goals or purpose other than simply to be. Nothing in the external world could provide the same spiritual contentment in which my soul was bathed; this state was incomparably superior to and far more fulfilling than anything the world had to offer. I was fully dead to the world, and I did not care about it in the least. I was fully content in God and with God alone. Thus, I came to feel that God had listened to and answered my inner cry from early September.

I continued night and day with my love-infused, prayerful aspirations, anchored by my faith in God and Jesus. Soon, something began to stick. At first it was very subtle, but as the weeks rolled on it lingered with me into activity. I felt a thread of continuity continually connecting me with an unchanging inner sphere of resplendent spiritual awareness, unabated by any circumstance. I would enter this sphere and dissolve all sense of "I-ness." This sensation persisted throughout sleep; it lasted into my waking state. It was as though the spiritual part of me witnessed my body sleeping, then witnessed it going through the various activities of life when I was awake.[40] I never lost touch with my spiritual core; it never left me.

In this manner, I experienced a dual consciousness, whereby I was simultaneously a detached witness and also a participant in life.[41] I identified with myself as a third-party onlooker. Although my perception was divided into watcher and watched, later this division broke down; my two selves rejoined, re-fused back together.

As detailed in Appendix III, I strongly felt my sensation of "I" was located above my head, and I referred to this inner sphere of "I-ness" as the "orb of silence." My challenge at first was to maintain this silence during periods of activity, and this initially caused me conflict as it required massive, sustained effort to sustain. But soon, a deafening silence became my primary nature, as this tension had resolved. My earlier struggles and periods of questioning and searching had fallen off by themselves. I felt I could now simply *be* without any worries; I no longer needed to push myself as before. I remained in a continually calm, unflustered state, which I felt at all times. I experienced unending joy when situated within my entrancing inner orb.

I would visualize the orb of silence as a tangible entity into which I could enter with a firm command of "relax." I would force my inner being into the orb, and I ruthlessly excluded all thoughts, mentations, emotions, and mental images, which remained outside. I came to identify with the orb; my "I" became one with it. I then expanded the orb outward as if on waves of infinite love, extending in all directions. By doing so, my "I" felt entirely anonymous and without any specific location; no separation existed anymore. My localized "I" dissolved into infinity, and "I" became one with all.

As mentioned above, over time, an ember of this orb began to glow while my body slept. My infinite "I" was this ember. Thus, my witness-consciousness strangely never slept, never turned off. I was never "involved" in situations; I felt totally detached, like a neutral observer. All things I encountered reflected off me. They weren't unreal—they existed, but apart from me. And yet, this "me" that existed apart from all things was at the same time their essence. There was no fundamental difference in the essential connection between me, the perceiver, and whatever object I perceived. We were one.

This dazzling awareness was far more vivid and real than anything experienced in ordinary consciousness. Its essence was composed of an inexhaustible boundless ocean of pure love. As I carried on with my prayers, I would at times express deep remorse upon the realization that, when growing up, I had lost the capacity to feel this fathomless divine love. But during this exalted time, I was suffused continuously in this palpable love, a love that was unrestricted in its scope and unlimited in its distribution. When this loving awareness engulfed me, I was dumbfounded; I couldn't understand why *I* was being showered with it. I became overwhelmed with heartfelt outpourings of gratitude toward God, toward Jesus. This brought about in me a state of childlike awe and wonder. The more I drank of this love, the more I discovered there was of it. I came to realize that this infinite divine love formed the very matrix of the universe and encompassed all things known and unknown.

The Royal Lichtenstein
Quarter-Ring Sidewalk Circus

On Thursday, December 19, 1974, a traveling troupe of three male performers calling themselves the Royal Lichtenstein Quarter-Ring Sidewalk Circus set up their show on our high-school campus. I joined around three dozen students, who had gathered during lunchtime to watch their midday performance, which was a delight. I laughed and reveled in their magic tricks, juggling routines, animal acts, antiestablishment comedy, and savvy light-handed preaching. But on that fateful day, I looked around and realized that no one saw what I saw. While many laughed at the performance, many were also caught up in their own worlds—rushing between classes, mentally preoccupied, unable to experience fully the joy of the moment. For some reason, this rattled me to the core, so much so that something inside of me collapsed. On that fateful day, I realized that I was alone, completely alone. No one shared my experience. Not one person. Not only my joyful experience of the circus, but, more important, I realized with open eyes that no one shared my inner spiritual experience. For the first time, it strikingly occurred to me that my previous sense that others participated in the same spiritual epiphany as mine was an illusion, a complete out-and-out illusion. I realized that my inner state wasn't accepted and that it couldn't be shared. In retrospect, this realization had begun simmering under the surface for the previous two or so weeks, but on this day it erupted full force. This startling insight imploded at the deepest level of my being and overcame me. I began to cry. I simply broke down in front of everyone assembled there.

The Royal Lichtenstein Circus performance in October 1975 at the University of Memphis (featuring Nick J. Weber)

Shortly thereafter, a colorful figure emerged from the circus backdrop and approached me. He was dressed in Tudor-era clothing and wore white face makeup. Looking like a cross between Jethro Tull's Ian Anderson[42] and William Shakespeare, he reassuringly clasped my upper arm. Then he spoke.

"Hey, I'm the clown. What's going on?"

"They can't see what I see!" I tearfully exclaimed.

After pausing a moment, he replied, "Not everyone can see magic. Not everyone has the gift to experience wonder."

I countered, "But I can't *share* what I see. I feel all alone."

He again paused before speaking these words. "If you experience the beauty and joy of life, that's a special blessing. It's a kind of innocence. Maybe you've been graced to see what others can't see, to carry this gift inside you."

I looked at him; he smiled at me. I said, "Yeah, maybe."

He concluded, "God reveals his wonders at all times, but most people are blind to them. Yet miracles occur around us constantly. That's the reason for the circus—to make others aware of the miracles of God."

**Students watch circus performers at the student union—
Tallahassee, Florida (from 1985, cropped from original)**

He looked at me with a look of utter sympathy. "Okay?"

No longer crying, I responded, "Okay." He smiled, then walked away and disappeared back into the circus.

I later learned that the clown was a Jesuit priest—Father Nick J. Weber, SJ, who subsequently resigned from the priesthood in 1993.[43] His beneficent words, which resound in me to this day, provided consolation that assuaged my disillusioned spirit. His succinct, solicitous remarks had the effect of affirming the validity of my spiritual experience. Though our chance meeting was short, its

61

effects were revelatory. He was the only adult who saw the essence of my being and my guileless spirit, and who accepted me at face value without judging me. How ironic it should be a traveling circus clown—an archetypal figure that can see beyond our personas and draw forth the unguarded innocence within us—who understood an all-too idealistic seventeen-year-old, and compassionately gave him permission to be himself. That brief empowering encounter, however improbable, conferred on me a priceless, lifelong gift.

But nothing could shore up my outer life. For the first time since my spiritual awakening began, I realized on a primal level just how isolated and truly alone I was. I knew as early as September 13 that I tended to be "non-social because of [my nonconformist attitude]." I wrote on December 4, "It is so hard for me to be who I am in front of people. I can only be who I am by myself." But this isolation had finally gotten under my skin. This wasn't because I didn't enjoy solitude, but rather because of the sense of alienation it produced. I felt myself an outcaste, almost a social pariah. I could not share my inner experience with even one other soul. Further, I had no support from my usual authority figures. No validation from my religious teachers, who should have provided spiritual direction. Practically no understanding from parents or friends. No context for my spiritual experience. And no future, because I had no footing on which to stand. I could not integrate my First Awakening experience into my daily activities on account of my uncompromising attitude. I did not even attempt to combine the two; this thought never once occurred to me.

There is a noticeable contrast between the combined months of October and November—the most intense period of my awakening—and the time from shortly after December 5 to mid-December, which was when my inner frustrations percolated and clearly precipitated my December 19 breakdown. Even my writings show a decisive change in style, insofar as I no longer wrote what I was directly experiencing, but instead I begin to write *about* what I had experienced. This is a subtle but pivotal change, revealing that, because I was able to objectify my own experience beginning in mid-December, this same experience was now in the past tense. Indeed, around this time I revealingly wrote, "I do not know if the mental state achieved previously can be duplicated again."

On approx. December 9, I wrote, "I am simply going crazy ... I have got to get out of this place." On December 12, I further wrote, "It is getting to the point where I could explode like an atom bomb at times. I long for freedom ... This whole authoritarian society is driving me insane!! ... Everything is so ... hopeless. My spirit is in bondage."

There is no question that I yearned for nature and bemoaned the fact that I could not escape this "living hell of a city" (December 7). "The city is repressive to the soul of man. ... I want to go somewhere quiet and seclusive. ... When I am alone, there is no timetable or schedule or responsibility" (December 12). On December 14, I wrote that I was "tremendously depressed." Of course, December 19 marked the final shard that cut my soul to the core; my emotional outpouring that day released much pent-up angst that I could no longer contain.

My idealistic bubble had burst; my dreams were shattered. I'm unsure if there was a specific event or a culmination of several different events that caused this inner crisis to foment and crest, but it was intense enough not only to halt, but to reverse my spiritual progress. I believe, then, that my spiritual experience peaked around December 6 to 12, when the last flashes of my unitive vision coursed through my consciousness, then it declined thereafter, at which time I slackened off on the previous intensity of my practices and soon after mostly gave up the combined meditation, prayer, and Bible-reading routine that I had followed since September. However, I never gave up my ideals of universal love and peace. On December 22, I wrote, "I want to bring people back to an age of innocence: no worry, no problems— the HERE and NOW." Still, I could neither share nor carry out these ideals. This proved to be the one chink in my armor. My spiritual vision of living in a world filled with love and peace had been crushed. The tug of war between heaven and earth was ending, and the stronger gravitational pull of earthly affairs yanked me from my celestial palace back into the stark, harsh world of human beings.

I felt totally deflated. My heart was broken. Reality set in, and I could not reconcile my inner world with the outer world, so I simply short-circuited. Hell hath no fury like a mystic scorned, and so, with a scorched-earth attitude of devil-may-care reckless abandon, I intentionally subverted all worldly plans for my future and refused to make any efforts to conform. Implacably defiant, I was content to suffer the consequences, come what may. (Looking back, I probably should have joined a monastery.) As my inner world too went down in flames, my defeated spirit looked on in horror, shedding bitter tears at the incalculable loss of contact with my spiritual self—the real me—on this indelible date of December 19, 1974, the saddest day of my young life. David Bowie perfectly captured my mood in his soaring and ultimately triumphant lyrics from "Wild Eyed Boy From Freecloud," which provided solace to my troubled soul.

My extreme, unyielding approach proved both a blessing and a curse. On the one hand, it enabled me to experience firsthand this wondrous state; but on the other hand, it made it impossible for me to implement my realizations in the real world. This and every similar roadblock I encountered showed me in no uncertain terms that I could not sustain my spiritual experience in the world of humans.[44] These sobering realizations, which dawned on me more as intuitions than reasoned conclusions, signaled the beginning of my separation from the invisible blessings that had carried me since September.

Even more consequential, because of the all-around lack of support I received from others, a seed of doubt had been planted in my mind. It grew to sabotage the single most meaningful experience of my life. Except for a solitary pivotal individual—a sympathetic priest/clown who arrived on the scene at the eleventh hour—not one significant person believed me. Worse, I began to believe their disbelief. This became my Achilles heel. In a complete reversal of my mood from September, when I threw off all chains and ruthlessly shunned the opinions of others, I now capitulated. I had opened the door just a crack by allowing their opinions to influence me, but I found I could not shut it again. Perhaps by thinking that if I compromised myself by jettisoning my spiritual mindset and adopting others' level of understanding I could somehow please them and cause them to accept me, I gave in, not realizing that by doing so, I would still be spurned. And so, instead of living evermore in a state of childlike innocence as I had visualized, I began rejecting my own spiritual realizations. Exhibiting an extraordinary and ultimately ruinous lack of judgment, I started believing that *I* was living an illusion, and that other people's reality was the real one. I was being evicted from Paradise, and by tacitly collaborating with my detractors, I materially assisted in facilitating my own expulsion.

When St. Peter walked on water to meet with Jesus on the turbulent Sea of Galilee, he was overcome with fear, and he started to sink,[45] whereupon Jesus immediately saved him from drowning, accompanied by a powerful rebuke: "O you of little faith, why did you doubt?"[46] Similarly, when I lost my faith, I began falling from the sublime revelation I had been given. I, too, could have turned to Jesus, as Peter did. But I committed the one unforgivable sin, which I repent to this day. At that critical juncture in my spiritual awakening, God gave me a personal test of faith. However, I did not turn to Jesus, as I had so many times in the previous three months. Instead, I turned to the world and sought its approval, choosing to listen to and—far worse—heed its collective, disparaging opinion at the expense of the lone supportive voice of Jesus.

Hence, I failed my test.

~~~~~~~~~~~~~

Years later, this brought to mind the words of *Peter Pan* author J. M. Barrie: "the moment you doubt whether you can fly, you cease for ever to be able to do it."[47] Sure enough, in the same instant when I doubted my own experience and lost the courage of my own convictions, my faith was shattered, and I lost access to the treasure that had been bestowed on me. At that very moment, my First Awakening experience started crashing to the ground.[48] And so, by paying attention to the naysaying of others and going so far as to imbue their dismissive words with credibility, I forfeited the one complimentary passage I had been granted in this lifetime to visit Eden and to be chauffeured on a magical tour through its many wonders.

From that point forward, I began breathing the air of mortals. My ego was returning, and I was headed earthbound fast. The uneasy descent lasted around two months, as my waning spiritual realization tauntingly lingered. As the spiritual portal continued to close, I rapidly lost touch with my soul. On that fateful day in December 1974, when I gave up believing in the reality of my own experience, my spirit began dying a slow death. To restate the words of poet Robert Frost, I thereupon chose the road *more* traveled by, which subsequently "made all the difference"[49] in my life.

During my spiritual awakening, my being had been rewired to withstand the energy of the Eternal. But when I lost contact with my spiritual essence, I was left hanging in midair—a stranger to both the divine and material worlds, not quite at home in either. I began wandering through an interior wilderness. Shaken from my foundation and realizing my grave mistake, I sought to return to my spiritual home—the only place where my soul could thrive. However, what had been given freely during my awakening, I now had to seek. Commencing in early 1975, I set out on a quest to recover my squandered treasure, a quest which continues to the present day. At that time, barely eighteen years old, I sought to reclaim my personal heaven, to reacquire what I had lost, and to consciously resurrect this unearthly experience that was gifted to me by God and once again establish it within my soul.

Bronze statue of Peter Pan located in Kensington Gardens, London

Afterthoughts

After this autumn 1974 narrative ended, I decompressed from my fallen mystical experience. I weathered many adjustments—and maladjustments—to life afterward, including facing my share of psychological and secular struggles. My spiritual experience forever affected and informed my life, both in terms of work and career, as well as relationships and lifestyle. I never "recovered" from my extramundane encounter. My experience had so profoundly conflicted with the prevailing view of reality that this discord created an undercurrent of alienation which underscored many of my ensuing undertakings in life. Over the succeeding decades, I spoke of my awakening to only a handful of people; my extreme guardedness about sharing such a private, sacred, and atypical experience compounded my sense of isolation. Amid this aftermath and fallout, however, I tried to remain true to the vision that was imparted to me during my First Awakening.

Starting in 1975, I would read accounts of analogous mystical experiences from different religious traditions, both Western and Eastern. I learned of similar experiences, especially from books on Christian mysticism, Hinduism, Sufism, Taoism, and Tibetan Buddhism. This gradually allowed me to begin placing my own spiritual awakening in perspective. I realized that my experience was not unique; I was just an ordinary kid undergoing an extraordinary experience. It was "nothing special"[50] as influential Sōtō Zen Master Shunryu Suzuki might have observed. It fell right within the bell curve of what many struggling mystics went through. Consequently, it was certainly nothing to boast about, especially because I could neither sustain my experience nor integrate it with my daily life. Instead, I lamented its loss, and I realized that a far more difficult journey would be needed to regain it.

By the same token, I do not intend to downplay or devalue the exceptional nature of my experience. Neither do I intend to imply that mine was a common occurrence. It was not. Few people experience these rare states of consciousness. I was incredibly graced. However, I unequivocally did not want to toot my own horn, which runs contrary to all cautionary spiritual teachings about not inflating one's ego, including Jesus' series of admonitions (Matthew 6:1–6, 16–18).

I underwent many additional inner experiences, which are described in Appendix II. However, as I emphasize below, these phenomena have nothing to do with genuine spiritual realization.

Finally, I learned four principal lessons from my First Awakening. First, it affirmed for me the authenticity of spirituality and the validity of the mystical experience. Second, it proved to me that following the spiritual path and realizing God were the primary goals of life. Third, it taught me never to lose faith in the conviction of my own experience, regardless of what others think. And fourth, it revealed to me that anyone can realize the truths of spirituality if they want them badly enough; the spiritual path is never for an elite few.

I hope to continue my post-First Awakening narrative in a future volume. Over the years, perhaps not surprisingly, I've taken an arms-length approach to much of institutionalized Christianity. Still, as I wrote in my book *The Deepest Silence*, "I was raised Catholic; I follow certain Catholic observances, and I am an advocate and practitioner of Catholic mysticism, which is a centuries-old authentic, vibrant spiritual tradition. I am grateful that the Church hosts these practices and upholds this heritage." However, I've come to embrace an interfaith, interreligious approach while maintaining my Christian/Catholic roots. Over the intervening decades, I've studied and earnestly practiced spiritual disciplines from many different religious traditions without abandoning my core Christocentric beliefs.

In doing so, I follow a well-established tradition trodden by several distinguished clerics, though I am neither an ordained member of the clergy nor would I be considered a well-known Catholic. There are certainly instances of prominent Catholics who remained Catholic while exploring different religions. The most notable example is Trappist Thomas Merton, who studied Eastern religions and promoted harmonious interfaith relations among religions. Jesuit Fr. John Harding wrote a two-volume *Religions of the World.* Dominican priest Richard Woods edited an anthology, *Understanding Mysticism.* Contemporary Jesuit Fr. Francis Clooney (Professor of Comparative Theology, Harvard Divinity School) has authored books on Hindu philosophy and practice while regularly saying Mass on weekends. Fr. Paul Jackson is a Jesuit who translated a Paulist Press book on Sufism. In terms of non-Catholics, perhaps the most respected and influential religious scholar of the twentieth century was Huston Smith, who remained a Methodist while studying under Hindu monastics and lecturing alongside the Dalai Lama. Smith penned the bestselling work on comparative religion, *The World's Religions*, a classic in the field.

[Note: In this and the subsequent three paragraphs that close this chapter, I have retained the narrative from my novel *Dialogues With the Lord of Time.*] I once met with Father Christopher and described a few seemingly unusual phenomena I then experienced, such as the sensation of walking on air, or feeling a continuous pronounced inner warmth in my upper torso. Father did not deny their validity, stating there are "esoteric lexicons" in most religious traditions that describe various "technologies of the soul." These lexicons and technologies help to map out and explain the interior spiritual terrain. They assist a person in navigating the varied experiences often encountered when unfolding these relatively uncommon states of consciousness.

In addition, the meditation technique I stumbled on differed from Father Christopher's method in that I concentrated on an object to still my wandering thoughts, typically a biblical passage or music, and I concurrently summoned up and utilized a massive amount of effort and willpower to forcefully control my mind. Father Christopher recommended the former—focusing on a home object—but he discouraged the latter. While both approaches require single-minded dedication and commitment, mine was a particularly arduous practice, which is why I believe Father didn't promote it.

~~~~~~~~~~~~~~~

During one of my early visits to see Father Christopher, I met with him privately and related the following. "Father, I underwent a spiritual experience more than fifteen years ago that transformed my life. It centered around Jesus. It was joyful beyond words. No one understood it, least of all me. All I wanted to do was to live perpetually in that state. But the world didn't support me and what I was going through, so I lost my faith and subsequently I lost my experience, which I've deeply mourned all these years. I've been trying ever since to recapture it."

Father immediately responded, "First of all, you never lost that experience. You were put in touch with your true spiritual nature. Don't ever doubt for a moment that it can be experienced again once you rid yourself of the layers which now cover it. More important, it sounds like you yourself caused it to end because you lost your faith. You looked to the world to validate what you were undergoing, which was a mistake of youth. Remember the wise words of the Psalmist, 'It is better to take refuge in God than to trust in people.'[51] When you try to please others, especially in matters of spirituality, you will never succeed. You must henceforth regain the conviction that your experience was genuine and ignore what the world thinks. You must fix your soul on God alone. Otherwise, this experience will elude you no matter how hard you try to re-establish it."

APPENDIX I

Eternity at Evolution Lake

"I would say that the trail doesn't change people at all. What changes people is that the trail is the means by which transformation takes place. ... It's what happens to you along the trail."[52]

–Yosemite Park Ranger Shelton Johnson

Evolution Lake Looking South over Evolution Basin

In early 1979, I chronicled my impressions of several imposing landmarks I encountered during my unearthly summer 1974 High Sierra wilderness adventure, focusing on my epiphanic experience at Evolution Lake (elev. 10,852 feet). These striking wonders of nature are situated above timberline at the leading edge of Evolution Basin in Kings Canyon National Park. In early 1979, I wrote the following:

> You look straight up and there, at Evolution Lake, stand these massive, towering palisades and skyscraping, jagged cliffs lined with multicolored walls of sheer granite, rising up and up, engulfing you with their overwhelming sense of timelessness. There you commune in silence. To stand among them, to walk below them, to gaze upward at them—

sublime worship, utter stillness. Nothing but horripilations and thunderous silence. Silence, silence. The gentle waters of Evolution Lake, where creation is an ageless phenomenon, beckon one to sit at its shores, to sit and *feel* the bottomless depth of this silence. The murmuring waters whisper eternity. An unspoken witness to the unmolded energy of life simultaneously bursting forth in all directions. The gigantic peaks—lone guardians, sentinels of time. Spiring skyward on sunlit shafts of primal rawness; arching across on craggy legs of infinity; moored in a beginningless past. One is caught in a timeless miracle. No longer to observe, but to *become* part of this wilderness. Each new moment you are unfettered, free. Never defined, never bound. No limits ... no limitations. No movement. An unparalleled, enveloping feeling: this overpowering, inexhaustible sensation of peace, peace, peace, filling your innermost soul. All sense of time is stopped. The mind thinks not. All self-reference comes to an end. No direction, no distance, no orientation. The raw experience of uncharted life.

APPENDIX II
Mystical Phenomena

In the present edition, I recount several additional mystical or psychical experiences that occurred to me during my First Awakening. Some might be considered standard psychic fare, while others decidedly border on the bizarre. I did not want these experiences to fall into the same category as those which are frequently overly dramatized and can stretch the boundaries of credibility, as are often depicted on popular television programs about alleged psychic or otherworldly occurrences. Then again, I can only report what actually, factually occurred to me. What follows are true accounts of the at-times strange experiences I underwent in late 1974, in no particular order.

Inner warmth. Further to what I wrote above about inner warmth, I felt this sensation of warmth equally distributed throughout my body, including my limbs, but it was especially pronounced in my upper front torso, around the heart and lower sternum region. I also felt warmth in the center of my feet when I would lie down meditating with my feet slightly propped up. This warmth was self-generated. This inner heat buoyed my fantasy of living in the Sierra, as I felt—rightly or wrongly—that this self-sustaining inner warmth would help me to survive in bitter cold temperatures.

A few years later, I would read of similar instances of thermal generation occurring around the heart area or elsewhere in the body during periods of intense, focused meditation, as documented in the Orthodox Christian and Tibetan Buddhist traditions. Tibetan practitioners sometimes consciously attempt to induce this state by performing a certain practice, which they term *tummo.*

Walking on air. I'll also expand on my brief mention above about "walking on air." In one of the most vivid experiences that occurred to me, one day I was walking along the first-floor corridor of my high school, headed east toward the double-door egress. Suddenly, with no advanced warning, I felt incredibly light, like I was partially floating, as if, during each stride, I actually paused midair before my feet returned to the ground. Now, no one walked up to me and exclaimed, "I just saw you levitating!" So, I maintain this occurrence was strictly my own subjective perception, allowing for the fact that my sensation of midair suspension could have been so subtle that it couldn't readily be detected. However, at the conclusion of this interlude, when I emerged eastbound from the building and began to descend down the several steps that led to ground level, I seemingly bounded off the top step and felt as though I were flying, as if my body were suspended in a momentary state of weightlessness, and I briefly floated while in midair and was escorted in slow motion to the landing below. My experience was akin to watching an astronaut leaping on the moon. This entire sequence of events remains a vibrant memory to this day; the experiential sensation of hanging in midair is unforgettable.

Seeing inside others. On some occasions, I actually saw other's inner states, like looking inside a glass display case. I felt their feelings and knew their thoughts, as if I were attuned to them by a direct connection, and we were on the same inner wavelength. When they spoke, I often saw people's words as picture images etched in my own mind. I came to perceive their thoughts as vivid glowing images, not as disconnected choppy mental patterns. In addition, and apart from my projecting my inner state onto others, I could often tell by simply looking at other people if they "knew" the spiritual reality firsthand when, for example, watching them speaking on TV.

Lightness of body. Relatedly, my body felt light, never heavy. I never felt burdened by it or incapacitated by any physical issue. On the contrary, I had tremendous energy, which I believed was imparted as a result—a side effect—of my deep meditations. In the context of yoga, my meditations produced an abundance of prana, or energy.

Posture. My posture underwent a change. I involuntarily began standing or sitting as erect as possible. I couldn't extend myself enough; I was stretched out at all times. I stood so straight that I felt my back ache; at times, my spine literally hurt. I later believed that my upright posture reflected my inner state, wherein I was freed of all heretofore dominant emotional complexes and I exuded utter confidence and self-esteem.

Breath. I also couldn't get enough air into my lungs. I breathed deeply, inhaling and exhaling at capacity, with no conscious effort to do so. My full respirations, too, hurt at times, as I was accustomed to relatively shallow breathing before my spiritual experience.

74

Air withdrawn from lungs. I underwent two, perhaps three of the most frightening possible events wherein the air was involuntarily pulled from my lungs. These occurred during the middle of the night. I awoke from sleeping on my back. An ember of my spiritual consciousness remained lit. I suddenly felt seized by an overpowering force. I couldn't move. I felt cold. I thought to myself, "I'm dying." I was in the grip of the most intense, desperate fear, as the breath was forced out of my lungs, like I was being winded. My limbs went limp; I lay helpless and immobile, like Jell-O. I felt I was disappearing! My self-consciousness was being sucked into this all-consuming vortex. I could not resist; I was completely paralyzed.

In keeping with my biblical context at the time, I felt the Devil was gripping me, and I felt fear, terror, and panic. I thought to myself, "I'm unable to move. I am losing all awareness [just like going under when administered nitrous oxide]. I am going to die! I must cry out; I must fight this; this is evil! I will not survive. I must ... (fading in and out of consciousness) ... I must fight ... (fading, fading) ... I must grab hold ... (fading) ... I must FIGHT, must LIVE."

I fought like never before, mustering up whatever strength I had. "I cannot die. What about my parents!" I faded in and out, and I was nearly overpowered. But I somehow managed to gather up all the life force within me, and I made the most intense effort I had ever made to break free, to emerge from this struggle. Somehow, I survived. One time, I came out of this with what seemed a yell, but was actually a faint moan. Afterward, I was thoroughly exhausted, utterly drained, yet calm. Then, I returned to sleep. Of these experiences, I told no one.

I later learned this was potentially similar to a *nirvikalpa samadhi* experience, which I prevented from occurring. In Hindu nomenclature, *nirvikalpa samadhi* is a heightened state of spiritual consciousness wherein all self-awareness is utterly effaced. Sri Ramakrishna is the only mystic known to have experienced this state for a six-month stretch; someone mysteriously came to him and forced food into his mouth so he wouldn't die. But I don't recall him mentioning having air withdrawn from his lungs.

Tibetan practitioners attempt to transfer their consciousness upward through the vertex, but this act is performed at the moment of death. Emanuel Swedenborg could place himself in a state of suspended animation and slow his breathing. So could certain Japanese Buddhist monks who engaged in the now outlawed practice of *sokushinbutsu*, an exquisitely prolonged form of self-mummification. Hindu yogis, such as Sadhu Haridas and Professor Yashpal, have voluntarily undergone vivisepulture for hours or days on end, and, as has been documented, survived. But the physiological act of having air violently withdrawn from the lungs is a nearly unique occurrence in the literature. Swami (aka Paramahamsa) Yogananda provided perhaps the only detailed account in his *Autobiography of a Yogi* I have read of having air withdrawn from the lungs, which paralleled my experience.

Speech and hearing. The way I spoke also changed. When speaking, I unconsciously inflected several different tones and volume changes. My speech became very smooth and, as far as I could determine, mellifluous. I spoke more softly, and I could hear myself speak much more clearly, as never before, because my mind was no longer cluttered with the usual thoughts, desires, emotions, and egotistical ruminations that would otherwise constantly occupy it. All such contents were emptied, thus there was no commotion inside my head to compete with my own voice. I listened more carefully and was in touch and in tune with myself. Others never mentioned anything to me about the new way I spoke and communicated, so my experience could have been only subjective.

Inner sound. I would hear a high-pitched ringing in my inner ear that was neither caused by tinnitus nor any other kind of hearing ailment. This phenomenon is known in Hinduism as perceiving the *anahata nada*, or unstruck sound—the *pranava*, commonly referred to as "OM." During very deep states of meditation, this sound would become deafening, which again provided another built-in internal focal point of concentration. As far as I can determine, this inner OM sound resonated at a frequency of approx. 1,411 hz., or F6-plus-17 cents. And, moving up one octave, it equally resonated at 2,822 hz., or F7-plus-17 cents.

Clear eyes. My eyes became crystal clear, possibly because of the tremendous prana coursing through my system. This marked one of the very few occasions when I felt self-conscious about my appearance. With my eyes of clarity, as mentioned above, I hesitated to look others directly in the eye. I was concerned that they might see the spiritual madness that had overtaken me.

Visions of inner lights. I routinely meditated with my eyes closed. As my mind sunk deeper and deeper into a state of unperturbed concentration, I began perceiving, in my inner vision, a display of slowly oscillating multicolored lights—numerous, ever-changing, glowing forms of color, which I found fascinating. I would focus on these intensely beautiful kaleidoscopic patterns of light and use them as an aid to my meditation session. I would try to find their source. I later learned my practice was similar to a yogic practice called *trataka*—staring undistractedly at an object for protracted periods of time in order to concentrate the mind. I became engrossed with this psychedelic array of patterns and colors, which appeared vortexlike before my mind's eye. I had accessed my own inner world of streaming lights, which was far more interesting than the distracting sights and sounds of the world outside. In addition, these inner lights were fairly constant. I could see them when I was active if I focused my eyes interiorly and steadied my mind.[53]

Visions of entities. However, I can't say the images of frightful entities I sporadically saw during deep states of contemplation were interesting. At some point while meditating, I began to experience terrifying visions of hideous demon-like beings with grotesque distortions of human features. Some had arms coming out of their heads, some had long, misshapen fangs for teeth, some had freakishly protruding bellies. Years later, I would read that these were "lower astral entities"[54]—creatures from the nether regions. This experience frightened me, as one entity would appear successively after another, starting as a tiny dot in the distance in my mind's eye, then moving toward me with increasing size until that entity dissolved right in front of my closed eyelids, then the next would take its place. Each was different. They were both male and female. Yet, I was in such a deep state of concentration that I could not move; any inkling of movement was nearly impossible, so I simply observed them and tried to calm my mind of any fright. These visions often repeated themselves, much to my dismay.

White light. Another time I had a "white light" experience, so often recounted during near-death experiences. Only, I was wide awake. I was preparing to shower at home when, in my mind's eye, an intense but warm white light filled the entire spectrum of my field of vision. I am reminded of a verse from the Bhagavad Gita:

77

If the effulgence of a thousand suns were to shine forth simultaneously in the sky, such a display would be similar to
the splendor of that magnificent Being.

        –Bhagavad Gita 11:12 (author's rendition)

Seeing in the dark.[55] I recall my occasional ability to see in the dark.
Specifically, I was at times able to locate items in the dark, such as
placing the arm of my turntable on the groove of a vinyl record that
was located precisely between two songs. I could not attribute such
occurrences to my having memorized the location of various items.

Above the cranium. During the height of my experience, I felt my
"I" consciousness located well above my physical head. One writing
placed my "I" several inches above my head, another three feet, another records it at ten feet. Looking back with a fifty-year
perspective, I've concluded that all these estimates are true; this sensation would telescope in and out at varying lengths.

I remember once sitting on a concrete car stop in my high
school parking lot and telling Art and another friend, perhaps Patrick, that I clearly felt my "self" was hovering several feet above my
head. This vivid sensation grew into a continual out-of-body experience, as my "I-ness" came to be situated in what I called an "orb of
silence" positioned above my cranium.

Another related experience occurred when I would lie down,
inwardly absorbed. On several occasions, I felt my mind was being
sucked upward and backwards, and it repeatedly spun upside down,
which produced a slight but distinct vertigo.

Heart palpitations. Once, when meditating while lying on my
back with my Bible on my chest, I was expressing devotional
effusions to God and my heart began beating faster and faster. I
could not control it and make it stop, so I just witnessed it until it
subsided. This lasted several minutes. I am certain this was not due
to premature ventricular contractions or any acute heart condition.

While none of these phenomena were earth-shattering events, I later
took them as signposts to help confirm the validity of my experience.
However, I must emphasize that these phenomena have nothing to do
with genuine spiritual realization, which occurs when the ego is effaced. One should not get sidetracked by seeking psychic phenomena.

APPENDIX III

Loss of Innocence

Except for my Bible readings and the writings mentioned in Endnotes 3 and 11, I read very little during my First Awakening. But I wrote down many of my thoughts. I felt that I was called on to capture my experience through my writings. Many times I felt impelled to write by an inner compulsion that often went against my will. Much of what I wrote more closely resembled a journal than a mystical treatise, though it was not like a daily diary. I felt my writings allowed me to vent a thwarted need to share and communicate; writing also helped to steady and focus my mind.

The following is a lightly edited longhand writing from December 14, 1974—ominously, five days before my implosion at the circus event that took place at my high school. Upon reading through these pages fifty years later, it's not difficult to see why I crashed or that a crash was imminent or even inevitable. What I see revealed is an innocent young man clinging to his idealism, a noble idealism, which collided with reality to produce a bitter disillusionment. However, while I had allowed the world to crush my spirit, this did not prove in any way to be the twilight of my ideals and dreams.

I was involuntarily introduced to the system when I was four years old. And probably indirectly before that … So, I figure I grew up into the system with no say in the matter, until now anyway. I was indoctrinated into a society in which money appears to be the key to survival and presumably happiness … I never knew any limits as a kid either, and the ones that were placed on me were usually when I was doing something wrong (in others' eyes anyway). But more specifically, I distinctly remember through a number of experiences from my crib to grammar school what it would be like when I grew up. And it was kind of a neat dream or fantasy: everyone loved one another. Period. Stop. Simply that's all. Everyone talked with, joked with, and loved one another. There was spirit and joy. Everyone laughed. There was love everywhere. Everyone was the SAME!!

But as I grew up, I learned that there were ... people who believed different things than I was taught. [And I was taught they were different not because they didn't share the same underlying love, but] because of skin color, culture, height, eye color, shoe size, job. It had *not* been the world I had imagined. I feel I have been totally cheated with regards to how my soul and spirit once looked upon the world and how it actually is—little children getting [their] guts ripped apart because someone thinks it is safer for democracy, children of all ages starving to death because someone is not altogether placing himself in the other person's position. My air and my earth and my trees and my fields and amber waves of grain are now covered with insecticides; purple mountain majesties are now being made into resorts. And spacious skies, which one may have a hard time finding with skyscrapers and smog.

I see people getting sold, "Look like this person," "Be, smell, react, think like this person." I see a million billion trillion different studies and surveys to name, record, tag, and ultimately MURDER my animals and strip my earth in the meantime. I see new methods to destroy human beings being invented constantly in the way of cars, pollution, accidents, suicide, bombs—need I say more—anything mechanical, anything invented by man.

The earth is harvested of her fine crops daily for the goal of killing one another. And we pollute the moon and outer space.

I see students and Blacks getting beaten up for voicing complaints of discrimination and asking for change. I see people getting murdered, assassinated, bought, sold, stamped, sealed, and filed constantly. I hear screams for change and a silent answer that is not listening.

My senses have been considerably (I hope not irreparably) dulled because of insecticides and smog and noise from traffic and bulldozers and airplanes and people yelling at one another using horns of various kinds. Guns for protection.

Money for survival. What is the end? How far are we going and where are we going?

This is a living hell for me and I am not going to grow up into it, because I remember what the potential for love was and what it actually is. I cannot conscientiously support a country either financially or morally that kills people, the animals and earth for fun and/or profit and for reasons I just know are wrong without having to explain. I don't think anyone (family, friends) knows what's going on inside me except me, so the only person I can live with who has complete understanding of me is me.

Although I feel cheated, it is for a selfish reason, for in the process I have learned a great deal about hunger and death and their causes. Hiroshima and Kent state. Whales. Little children who are *born dying*. Pollution. The stripping of the earth of all her resources for streets and factories and skyscrapers and cars and bombs and stereos and 46,943 different variations of Captain Crunch breakfast cereal, and preservatives in food made [using] insecticides, and changes in weather conditions and drought and plagues and disease and destruction and famine, and what about the little children who are going to be playing here in a hundred, two hundred, a thousand years from now?

Will there be zoos for everything from the three last remaining species of animals (dogs, cats, and hamsters) to the last tree?

> Born: 463 B.C.
> Lived: Until industry, about 1850–1900
> Died: Because of smog and insecticides, 1984
>   (because of man)

How many coyotes do we kill because they endanger the sheep and cattle, which are killed because people like to eat the muscle or tail or arm or tongue of the animal, then wear what's left as a belt or a shoe?

If everything [were] as I imagined it to be when I was a kid, I wouldn't feel the way I do. I feel bad because of all that

[I've] mentioned. I feel good because maybe more people will feel the same way I do and we can silently change things.

If I leave this place (with a diploma and basically what other people expect me to be), it will be for my own sanity (maybe I should be locked up in an asylum or put away somewhere). What I want is a world like I feel was promised to me when I was a kid—without death and people blowing one another up. The way I want to have this world would be through love or through was I felt was love, and the end result could be Paradise II.

I don't want to "become" a doctor or a lawyer or a this or a that. I want to be ME first and before anything else. I don't want to live up to other people's expectations of what they think I *should* be. I want to be happy and I want to thrive and grow in a world with love. I want my freedom. True, I can have and have had *internal* freedom, but when I open my eyes, they get irritated with the "real world" because of pollution and death. So, if the only place I can live is in my head, I don't think it would hurt if I did leave. The big thing that is holding me back is not so much anything else except my own conscience. If I did go, it would be for a selfish reason (*my* sanity), and I would like someday to repay all the people who helped shape my life and to make the world, which has death and pollution, thrive on love as the only economy, politics, and society. But in the meantime, I'll dream and hope I don't explode.

It will always be in the back of my mind that in the loss of innocence I realized that I probably have hurt some people, friends, family, whatever. I can only hope they will someday forgive me if I have, and realize I was only searching for something I had long forgotten—love. The time I seem to like the best nowadays is when everyone else is sleeping. It gives me a chance to listen to myself without all the requests, responsibility, airplanes, cars, visual pollution.

I think the worst murder, rape, and pollution in our society is the selling of the soul and spirit for the sake of mass production and efficiency. Wants, desires, needs—they are all pre-programmed from everything from Monday Night Football and newspapers to advertising and violent films, reserved vacations (why does one have to wait fifty weeks out of the year for two weeks of peace of mind?).

I cry a lot when I see my friends grow up into this madness because I feel that I am all alone in my cause for love. I never want to grow up. I want to start my childhood over again in a universal community of love, like I thought it would be. ... I want the wonder, the awe, the never-ending curiosity of a child. The concepts I had when I was a kid of time, distance, space, sound—I want my awareness back. ... That's how it was in Paradise, I think, I hope, I pray.

~~~~~~~~~~~~~

Again, on January 12, 1975, while still age seventeen, I reaffirmed my ideals in another short writing. I am reminded that, in the original *Peter Pan* novel, the Lost Boys grew up, whilst Peter chose to remain in Neverland.

I'd like to live in a world of peace and freedom where everyone lives as one in love and concern for one another, the planet we live on, and the other forms of life it fosters. A world where there is no such thing as greed. A world of consideration for one another in which there are no takers at the expense of another's happiness. A world where the sometimes confused, troubled, and hostile world of 1975 is non-existent. Right now, my world is a hypothetical one, but I hope to see it become a reality, and darn soon for the sake of all of us and our children, and their children, and the present and future survival of all humanity in harmony with each other and the planet we live on.

I'd like to see a world of Love
Peace Freedom Harmony for All
No war No rules No Takers No law
No people starving No one unhappy anymore
A society of love
An economy of hope
The politics of self
Without any limits whatsoever
But it seems to tell people this
I have To have money
And have my name in the paper
Can't people realise that
Smog and cement are wrong
Breeding animals in cages just to kill and eat
Power and Mind games
T.V., Corporations, Adds, Police, Schools
Jails, Kent State, Vietnam

January 3 1975

"I'd like to see a world of Love, Peace, Freedom, Harmony for All. No war. No rules. No takers. No law. No people starving. No one unhappy anymore. A society of love … An economy of hope … The politics of self — Without any limits whatsoever. But it seems to tell people this I have to have money and have my name in the paper. Can't people realize that smog and cement are wrong? Breeding animals in cages just to kill and eat. Power and Mind games. T.V., Corporations, Ads, Police, Schools, Jails, Kent State, Vietnam … "

John Roger Barrie
January 3, 1975

NOTES

[1] I had adopted a motto during the 1970s, said to have originated in New England, and which first became popularized during World War II: "Use it up, wear it out; make it do, do without." However, this attitude of frugality completely clashed with the winner-take-all, acquire possessions at-all-costs ethos of American capitalism. Then again, my hero was Henry D. Thoreau, not John D. Rockefeller.

[2] If pressed, I would add a fourth, honorary philosopher to this distinguished group, which recognizes the homespun, highfalutin thinkin' of American novelist and humorist Samuel Langhorne Clemens (1835–1910), better known by his more familiar pen name, Mark Twain.

[3] In 1973, I purchased *On the Brink of the Absolute* (1973) by American-born, Hindu-oriented Master Subramuniya (1927–2001) at Music Odyssey in West L.A. In 1974, I borrowed a library book from my high school, *The Teachings of the Compassionate Buddha* (paperback edition, 1955), edited by E. A. Burtt. I also recall watching occasional black-and-white episodes on TV that featured an engaging man espousing Eastern philosophy, possibly Alan Watts (1915–1973) or Richard Hittleman (1927–1991), or perhaps both.

I read of John Muir's incredible adventure atop a tree during a Sierra Nevada windstorm from his *Mountains of California*, which was stocked in our school library. On November 25, 1974, I hand copied a poem, *Freedom is Nature's Way* by Neal Fortin, from the Fall 1974 issue of *Backpacker* magazine at our library, which spoke directly to me. I would occasionally bring nature magazines to school and share them with one or two friends. But I did not read extensively during this time.

[4] From the documentary *High Sierra—A Journey on the John Muir Trail*.

[5] As I grew older, the realities of life served as a nonstop source of insidious pressure, aiming to burst the bubble of my innocence and idealism. I've always felt that I compromised by joining the system because of the incessant need to "make a living," though I never inwardly fully embraced the dominant hyper-consumerism mentality of the age and culture.

⁶ A decidedly Jesuit form of punishment, "jug" is derived from the Latin *jugum*, alternately *iugum*, meaning "yoke." The Sanskrit word *yoga* shares a similar etymological root. Jug was intended to yoke those who had committed punishable infractions under the submission of school authorities, who would then mete out commensurate sentences in order to extract reparation for the students' various behavioral misdeeds. Yoga, on the other hand, is intended to yoke the individual soul to God. I guarantee, we never sat in the lotus posture chanting "OM" during any session of jug that I had the misfortune of attending.

⁷ I will concede the genius, however unintentional, in one couplet by John Milton (1608–1674), from *Paradise Lost* (1667), Book I, verses 254–255:

> The mind is its own place, and in itself
> Can make a Heav'n of Hell, a Hell of Heav'n.

⁸ Yet, as a young child I suffered occasional attacks of fear of the dark, and I would become terrified of being alone through the long night. I suffered night terrors, and I would yell out for my mother when overwhelmed with fear. My best friend was my nightlight. I eventually outgrew this phase, which fortunately never morphed into a more crippling nyctophobia. But the exact opposite occurred during my spiritual awakening. I then craved solitude. Instead of fearing the night, I welcomed it, and I would seek solace in the thick blackness I had created around me.

⁹ It wasn't until the late 1990s when I discovered that my Bible-reading routine was virtually identical with a centuries-old Christian practice called *Lectio Divina* ("divine reading"), whereby a spiritual aspirant single-mindedly reads and intently reflects upon one Bible passage until their mind is fully absorbed in it, and they thereby become steeped in a state of deep contemplation.

¹⁰ I learned this from an article I had read in a magazine.

¹¹ I recall reading a section from a self-help book, which I don't remember how I obtained, called *Yoga for Men Only* (paperback edition, 1969) by chiropractor Frank Rudolph Young. I ignored the book's more grandiose topics and claims, and zeroed in on its discussion of the "Four Horsemen of the Mastabah," which pointed out the deleterious effects of the downward pull of gravity and the adverse

consequences of weightbearing. This made an impression, prompting me to lie down when meditating. (I also recall watching someone on television demonstrate meditation while lying down, possibly Richard Hittleman.) I would then intentionally relax my arms and legs, mentally starting at my feet and working up through every limb until they were completely relaxed. This supine position became my favored posture whenever I would meditate. Several months later, I discovered this position paralleled a posture from hatha yoga practices known as the *shavasana* or "corpse" pose.

[12] I've suffered from a lifelong allergic rhinitis condition, including annoying body-wide sensations of itching when in a predominantly quiescent state, such as when falling asleep or engaged in deep meditation, likely due to a histamine dump.

[13] Matthew 6:33.

[14] John 4:24.

[15] 1 John 4:8.

[16] Luke 17:21.

[17] Mark 12:30–31.

[18] Matthew 6:21.

[19] Matthew 6:24.

[20] Matthew 7:24.

[21] Matthew 4:19.

[22] When I took my high-school entrance exam, I scored "in the 99th percentile." As memory serves, my IQ score from my middle grammar school years was 135.

[23] Matthew 16:26.

[24] Mark 12:30–31.

[25] John 13:34.

[26] Matthew 7:12, Luke 6:31.

[27] Matthew 6:24.

[28] "For are you not of more worth than the clothes?" In essence, I felt invisible; clothes were a social nicety. I often felt I could go to school naked and not be noticed, but in retrospect, I'm glad I didn't attempt this. However, I truly felt I could move about unnoticed because "I" wasn't actually present; there was no one to be noticed.

[29] Luke 14:26.

[30] John 13:34.

[31] Around 1988, I dreamt a revealing dream: I was flying in a Superman costume, high above the atmosphere, free and ready to take on my calling in life. But when I looked behind me, there was my mother, flying in back of me, tagging along, dogging me. No matter which way I veered, I couldn't escape her. She would change her route to match mine. I couldn't get on with my life's work. Her trailing presence so dominated my efforts to navigate my flight path that it interfered with my ability to plan my life and achieve my goals.

[32] Lewis Carroll, *Alice's Adventures in Wonderland* (1865), Chapter V, "Advice from a Caterpillar."

[33] I could still drive when necessary, but it was an altogether different experience, as though someone else were at the wheel. Heavy traffic situations were the worst possible circumstances for me, creating anxiety. But during my First Awakening, I maintained my poise, shrouded by the love of God. When driving, I forced my body to relax while driving, similar to when meditating, and I was thereby able to maintain my experience even while driving and during other states of activity, although it certainly intensified when I was alone.

[34] During my awakening, I did not have any spiritual dreams, or visitations by or visions of spiritual beings. For instance, I never experienced a vision of Jesus. However, I once dreamt a lifelike dream in which a procession of radiant young men passed by an assembled crowd, which included me. We were sitting in chairs outside a Catholic church. The young men walked in unison. They were clad in white robes, and their faces shone a brilliant golden aura. These majestic beings were silent. They gazed straight ahead, never looking around, as if wholly preoccupied with God. We all knew they were followers of Christ.

In their midst was a chariot, which several of them carted along. When it drew near, a man stationed next to the crowd beckoned us all to stand in reverence. Seated on the chariot was the chief of this retinue, a noble, luminous young man with light-brown, medium-length hair, whose head was encircled by a magnificent golden aura. He, too, kept silent, inattentive to the crowd, as if inwardly transfixed on God alone. We were collectively awestruck and rendered speechless by this otherworldly procession as it moved past us.

I realized upon waking that I had witnessed an entourage of God's angels, led by a powerful, illustrious archangel.

[35] I recall a couple of occasions when I would stare intensely into my eyes while gazing in the mirror, but I would see no one familiar looking back; I literally lost the ability to recognize myself.

[36] Matthew 6:4.

[37] Elizabeth Barrett Browning, *Aurora Leigh* (1856), Seventh Book.

[38] Matthew 7:1–2.

[39] A year or two later, I learned this process was similar to the hallmark spiritual practice advanced by the nineteenth-century-born Hindu saint Ramana Maharshi, which he termed *Self Enquiry*.

[40] I would later read of the Hindu term *sakshi*, which means "witness" and is used to describe this witness-consciousness.

[41] I would later read of this phenomenon in what would become one of my favorite passages in the Upanishads:

> Two birds, inseparable friends, cling to the same tree. One of them eats the fruit of divergent tastes, the other looks on without eating.

[From the Mundaka Upanishad 3:1:1, adapted from (1) *The Sacred Books of the East, Vol. XV, The Upanishads*, Friedrich Max Müller (trans.), *The Mundaka Upanishad*, Third Mundaka, First Khanda, Verse One, (Oxford: Clarendon Press, 1884), p. 38; and (2) *Eight Upanishads, Volume Two*, Swami Gambhirananda (trans.), *The Mundaka Upanishad*, Third Mundaka, Canto I, Verse One, (Kolkata: Advaita Ashrama, 1958), p. 116 ("of divergent tastes").]

[42] Ian Anderson, the principal songwriter and frontman of the musical group Jethro Tull, which he cofounded in 1967.

[43] Nick J. Weber (b. 1939) penned his captivating adventures, which are depicted in his engrossing autobiography, *The Circus that Ran Away with a Jesuit Priest: Memoir of a Delible Character* (Indianapolis: Dog Ear Publishing, 2012).

[44] Relatedly, the great Hindu saint Sri Ramakrishna cautions that "the experience of the spiritual ecstasy shakes and sometimes shatters the body" (from *Teachings of Sri Ramakrishna* [Calcutta: Advaita Ashrama, 1934 edition], p.324). In a similar manner, my own mystical experiences may have taken an unseen toll on my health.

[45] Matthew 14:28–30.

[46] Matthew 14:31.

[47] J. M. Barrie, *Peter Pan in Kensington Gardens* (1906), Chapter II.

[48] Referencing a far less highbrow literary source than J. M. Barrie, my spiritual downfall also brought to mind an episode from the screwball 1960s sitcom *Gilligan's Island,* which I somehow recalled watching from childhood, and which evidently made an impression (thus proving that lessons in life can be gleaned anywhere). In this installment, Gilligan began flying from the roof of a hut using a pair of wings he fashioned from feathers. Until the Skipper, like a wet blanket, shouted to him from the ground below that he *cannot* fly, adding that to do so was impossible. Poor gullible Gilligan believed the omnipotent, confident Skipper more than his own experience. Sure enough, in the same instant when his faith had been shattered, Gilligan came crashing to the ground ... similar to when I had lost my faith and this killed my experience. (From "Will the Real Mr. Howell Please Stand Up?" from *Gilligan's Island,* Season Two, Episode 26, which originally aired on March 17, 1966. I was then nine years old.)

[49] Robert Frost, *The Road Not Taken* (1915).

[50] Shunryu Suzuki, with Trudy Dixon (ed.), *Zen Mind, Beginner's Mind* (New York: Weatherhill, First Paperback Edition, 1973), p. 47.

[51] Psalm 118:8.

[52] From the documentary *High Sierra—A Journey on the John Muir Trail.*

[53] Swami Sivananda of the Divine Life Society noted the occurrence of inner lights in his *Spiritual Experiences* (Sri Swami Sivananda, *Spiritual Experiences* [Uttarakhand: The Divine Life Society, First Edition, 1957], pp. 55, 64–65.)

[54] Sivananda, op. cit., p. 74.

[55] All my life I've been categorically unsuccessful whenever willfully attempting to perform psychic powers, whether bending spoons, moving objects (telekinesis), or psychically commanding other people to promptly respond to my emails. Whenever I've tried to predict a particular future outcome, usually the opposite occurs. The only times I've found when selected psychic powers have even minimally worked is when they occurred *through* me without my conscious effort.

I should note that the development of such powers is positively shunned in the Ramakrishna–Vedanta tradition wherefrom my teaching authorization is derived, and I counsel others accordingly. Historically, many Catholic spiritual directors also discourage psychic powers.

ABOUT THE AUTHOR

John Roger Barrie is the longtime literary executor of influential author, historian, and philosopher Gerald Heard (1889–1971), and the creator and publisher of geraldheard.com, online since 2002. He has overseen reissues of eighteen classic Gerald Heard titles. Previously, he served for many years as a regional freelance writer and editor.

For five decades, Mr. Barrie has practiced spiritual disciplines from a variety of different religious traditions, and he has studied with and received blessings from numerous spiritual teachers. Raised a Catholic, he has intentionally followed the spiritual path since 1974, branching out thereafter to embrace an interfaith approach all the while maintaining his Christian roots and practices.

His first published spiritual article appeared in 1981. His first book, the acclaimed spiritual novel *Dialogues With the Lord of Time*, was published in 2023, while *The Deepest Silence and Other Essays on Contemporary Spirituality* was published in 2024. He maintains a running blog on his website, *Explorations in Contemporary Spirituality*.

Mr. Barrie is honored to have a longstanding teaching authorization as a lay instructor in the respected, interfaith-oriented Ramakrishna–Vedanta tradition. His interfaith approach incorporates teachings and practices from many religions and spiritual paths. His emphasis on experiential spiritual realization and his firsthand familiarity with diverse spiritual traditions has imbued him with a fluent knowledgebase and practical outlook when addressing the subtleties of the mystical path. For more information, visit johnrogerbarrie.com.

John Roger Barrie lives in Northern California with his wife.

www.ingramcontent.com/pod-product-compliance
Lightning Source LLC
Chambersburg PA
CBHW060336130626
46553CB00003B/1008